Books by Todd and Jedd Hafer

TODD & JEDD HAFER

WAKE UP AND SMELL THE PIZZA

BETHANYHOUSE

MINNEAPOLIS, MINNESOTA

Library of Congress Cataloging-in-Publication Data

Hafer, Todd.
    Wake up and smell the pizza : 40 Tasty readings for a super supreme life / by Todd & Jedd Hafer.
        p. cm.
    Includes bibliographical references.
    ISBN 0-7642-0033-X (pbk.)
    1. Teenagers—Religious life. 2. Teenagers—Conduct of life. 3. Devotional calendars. I. Hafer, Jedd. II. Title.
    BV4850.H255   2005
    242'.63—dc22   2004020049

FOREWORD

First off, let me say that I agreed to do this foreword for one main reason: Jedd and Todd Hafer have a heart for the same thing I—and we as a band—do: teens.

Like Superchic(k), Todd and Jedd are constantly working to be relevant to teens today. I believe you have to do this by meeting teens where they are and trying to help them face the issues they deal with. The only way that you can know any of that is to talk with them.

I like the fact that Jedd and Todd knew that they needed to talk with teens, find out what their issues are, and find legitimate ways to help them.

In fact, the layout is one of the things that I really like most about this devotional. Todd and Jedd start with the issues first, and then they give advice and creative exercises to do. A big part of dealing with any issue is presenting something people can apply to their lives—a way to work on a problem or challenge through some sort of exercise.

The other great thing about this book is that it doesn't skirt any issues. It addresses some of the toughest topics there are: suicide, sexual temptation, body image, and depression.

There can never be enough devotionals, because teens will never stop changing and dealing with different issues. This devotional is fresh and new and has something for any teen anywhere. It will be great for independent study or group study. It's versatile and interesting! Good job, Jedd and Todd! And to you, the reader, enjoy!

Melissa Brock of Superchic(k)

TODD HAFER, a veteran writer with over twenty books published, is a senior editorial director for Hallmark, Inc., and lives with his family in Kansas.

JEDD HAFER is a comedian and speaker who has performed all over the nation. He is also a director at Children's ARK, a treatment center for troubled teens. Jedd and his family make their home in Colorado.

CONTENTS

INTRODUCTION

Divorce. Drugs. Teen suicide. Sex. Internet predators. We talked about all of this and more. It was another Wednesday night with a church youth group—maybe like one you belong to. We laughed a lot, a few people teared up, and at one point a teen asked to be excused from the group for a moment because she had to, and we quote, "take care of a wedgie problem."

After the evening ended—and the last pieces of cold pizza and cups of room-temperature Mountain Dew were scavenged—we handed out response cards to the attendees. This is a Hafer brothers tradition. We hunger for feedback. We want to know if we've connected with a group. We want to know what we can do better the next time. And we're insecure. On this particular night, the responses were rewarding, so positive that it was almost embarrassing. As we shuffled through our thick stack of three-by-five cards, we read comments like "Please come back soon," "You guys are hilarious," and "Please stay in touch."

Then, at the bottom of the stack, we found one dissenting reaction. The note was printed in a scrawling, scratchy, asymmetrical hand that had to be a guy's (because it looked like *our* handwriting). The feedback was terse and to the point: "Next time, bring more pizza."

At first, this seemed like a real buzz kill after basking in all the compliments, but we ended up laughing and marveling at how God does such a good job of pounding home lessons in humility—even using our favorite food as a hammer.

We didn't think much about the "Pizza Card" after that night—until it was time to start writing our latest book for teens and the adults who care about them. We were trying to come up with a theme, a "hook" as they call it in the publishing industry.

We knew what we wanted to do: Talk about what's fresh, what's hot. We wanted to deliver a devotional with the works. Then it hit us: Fresh, hot, deliver, the works. Pizza, of course.

"Okay," you might be saying, "I understand why you titled this book *Wake Up and Smell the Pizza*, but why write another teen devotional? Like brands of frozen pizza, don't we already have enough of them?"

Maybe. We know there are a lot of great teen-related books out there. We recommend many of them at the end of this book (check out the "Extra Toppings" section). But we couldn't think about things like market saturation or duplication of effort. We simply had to write this book.

Why? Because we care too much not to. We have worked with teens since we *were* teens. As high school students, we taught Sunday school classes to our peers. We led Bible studies—one in the biology lab of a public high school. Try to get away with that today.

Currently, Jedd's job is working with teens. He is a director at Children's ARK, a treatment center for kids who have run away, been abused, arrested, and/or kicked out of traditional schools or programs. (The average ARK kid has been kicked out of four other programs. And as for the "above average" kids, you might not believe it if we told you!)

Todd is a parent to two teenagers, a reality that still amazes and frightens him regularly.

We also work with school kids, church kids, sports teams—you name it. Bottom line: The teen world isn't just a book topic for us; it's our life.

Much has changed about teen life since our own middle school and high school years, but there is one constant: Being a teen is hard. Do you know that almost one-fourth of eighth graders have tried "huffing"— using household chemicals like paint thinner or type corrector to get high? Or that almost four million teens get infected with a sexually transmitted disease every year? (That's about equal to the combined populations of Montana, South Dakota, Wyoming, Alaska, Vermont, and

North Dakota!) Or that suicide is one of the leading causes of death among teens? Or that the 2003–2004 school year was the worst for school violence in a decade? School-related violence claimed forty-eight lives, more than the two previous school years combined. Want more cheery news? Millennials, people born in 1982 or later, are leaving churches by the millions.

Statistics like these are important to acknowledge, but we share them reluctantly. You see, sometimes when you talk about percentages and millions of people, the stats lose their personal meaning. And that cannot happen, because we are talking about individual human lives, and each one matters. When we walk through the halls of a middle school, for example, we look at the faces and it kicks us in the heart to think that about every fourth kid is risking his or her mental well-being—and even life itself—in a quest to get high.

So we didn't write this book for "the millions of teens out there." We wrote it for you, personally.

Maybe you're strong in your faith and have been able to avoid the tragedies and heartbreaks that invade many teens' lives. But you need encouragement and information to help you *stay* strong. And you want to be able to help your friends, some of whom are dancing with danger. We're here to help you.

Or maybe you feel your life is a mess. You're into things that would shock your parents if they knew. Perhaps, more tragically, they wouldn't care. We're here for you too.

If you're like most teens we meet, you're somewhere between the two extremes. Some areas of your life are under control, but you have a weakness or two. Secret temptations. Private but dangerous habits. You're being pulled in two different directions. It's like your heart is a chunk of meat that two starving dogs are fighting over. You're not sure which one is going to win. Dude (or Dude-ette), can we help you! We've been there.

You might be a concerned youth leader, parent, or teacher looking for a way to connect more closely with the teens in your life. You are looking for a resource. Maybe this is it.

We sincerely hope this book will be meaningful to you, whatever your situation. Not because of our impressive credentials (we don't have any; the only professional organization we belong to is the Subway Sandwich Club), but we do have a few things going for us. First, we truly want to offer encouragement and faith-based advice more than anything else. It's not important that you remember our names or write glowing reviews of this book on *Amazon.com*. We'd much rather you forget all about us, but remember the biblical principles and time-tested advice we'll be providing.

Second, we aren't the smartest guys in the world, but at least we realize that fact. Thus, this book isn't just a collection of our insights. If that were the case, it would be more like a pamphlet. So we relied on the wisdom and experience of people more qualified than we are. Some of them are authors whose books we recommend back in "Extra Toppings" land. (In fact, the section called "More Stuff to Chew On" might be the most valuable part of the whole book.)

Other insights came via teens from high schools, middle schools, churches, etc., who have helped us get a clearer picture of what it means to be a teen in the twenty-first century. So, thank you, students from Wasson High School, Doherty High School, Monticello Trails Middle School, Mill Valley High School, Colorado Springs Christian School, Pulpit Rock Church, The Children's ARK, Woodmen Valley Chapel, and Southwoods Christian Church. Thanks also to those of you who shared your hearts via our Web site, *www.haferbros.com*. This book wouldn't exist if not for you.

Also, we have enjoyed the humbling privilege of tapping the brains of some awesome colleagues and friends—see the "Acknowledgments" section for more info on these people.

Finally, we want to assure you—or perhaps warn you—that we don't duck difficult topics in the following pages. One of the reasons we wrote this book is that we have noticed a trend in Christian publishing to deny the realities of life in today's world or to quickly gloss over them. This doesn't work. If a teen is addicted to pornography, for example, it's feckless to say, "Just quit looking at the porn, dawg. Read Deuteronomy instead, and try to think of Moses or Elijah whenever temptation emerges." Indeed, that is advice entirely lacking in "feck."

If you believe that God is relevant to contemporary life (as we do) and that his Word is more than a quaint relic from a time unlike today, then you must trust that he will provide guidance for all areas of life. That means Internet pornography, substance abuse, eating disorders, suicide, you name it.

We are trying to convey that guidance in a way we hope you will find relevant, challenging, funny, and memorable. In short, we hope we can deliver.

And, by the way, to that guy in the youth group: Dawg, we *promise* to bring more pizza next time.

HOW TO USE THIS BOOK

Well, basically, you just read it and try to learn something. It's not complicated. But since we have a page to fill here, we should tell you about a few of the features and benefits of the book. (And if we say "features and benefits" one more time, or use any other bit of soul-less Corporate America jargon elsewhere in this book, you have our permission to throw corn dogs or the projectiles of your choice at us if we ever come to your town to speak.)

As you dive into *Pizza*, you'll see that each of the forty readings features an ingredient that will enrich your life in some way. The "meat" of each devo is a story, mini-essay, or interview that explores what the ingredient is, why it's important, and how to incorporate it into the mix of your life.

Next comes a "Slice of Advice," a Bible verse or quote related to the topic.

In some cases, a "Slice of Advice" will be followed by a brief rant titled "Please, Easy on the Cheese." Here, we will take on so-called pop-culture experts or expose myths that too many teens are buying in to.

Topping off each devo is a challenge called "Deliver on This." This is where you get practical. This is where you take what you've read and make it work in your everyday life, because the words we write aren't meant to just lie there on the page any more than a pizza is meant to sit in the box until the cheese gets rubbery and the crust fossilizes and not even your dog will eat it.

This is stuff to live out. Ideas to put into practice. You can work on one idea a week or go at a quicker pace if you wish. Every so often, we'll provide a "Time to Reheat It" section, in which we'll review what has gone before and allow you to reflect on how you've been doing with your "deliveries." So let's get started. We're at your door. We have something for you.

NOSE ART

Here's something fun to do next time you're in an art museum. Okay, we know what some of you are saying: There will be no "next time" you're in an art museum. In fact, there won't be a *first* time. But don't be too quick to say that. You might be walking around in a city someday and get lost and be forced to pop into a museum to ask for directions.

Or you might be right outside the doors to a museum when a sudden hailstorm hits—and you'll have nowhere else to go.

And, of course, some of you reading this actually might like museums and visit them frequently.

Whatever the case, here's your museum assignment: Find a large painting and stand as close to it as those burly museum guards will allow. Get your nose millimeters from the canvas if you can. Then stare really hard at the painting.

What you'll see, most likely, is an unintelligible mass of paint globs and brushstrokes. From this vantage point, you can't tell what the painting is supposed to represent. In fact, if you didn't know what you were looking at, you might not even be able to tell it's supposed to be a painting. It might look like a clown blew up—or threw up—on a slab of canvas.

To understand what the painting is about, of course, you have to take a few steps back. You have to take in the whole thing to see what the artist was trying to achieve. You must have *perspective* before things make sense.

You know where we are going with this analogy, don't you? That's right, our friend, art imitates life, and life is all about perspective.

Our first chapter is about perspective, because perspective will set the tone for this book, and your life. It will determine how you perceive what happens around you and to you. It will determine how you react.

We are convinced that so many of teens' life tragedies—from suicide to sexual promiscuity to running away from home—happen because teens and the adults around them lose their sense of perspective.

We don't want this to happen to you.

We're about to hit you with a key truth that will be vital to keeping your life in perspective, no matter what happens. It's a deep, profound truth, so you might want to write it down so you won't forget it. Here goes: Jesus loves you, this we know, for the Bible tells us so.

Pretty cool, huh? Somebody ought to turn that into a song or something.

And please don't dismiss those words just because they rhyme and you maybe heard them in Sunday school. Don't say, "Sunday school Jesus is just for little kids. He is not relevant to life in the twenty-first century."

Wrong. Jesus isn't just for Sunday school. He is By-Your-Side-on-the-Way-to-the-Crisis-Pregnancy-Center Jesus. He is Holding-Your-Hand-While-You-Clutch-the-Bottle-of-Pills-That-Could-End-Your-Life Jesus.

The Bible promises you that nothing—NOTHING—can separate you from Jesus' love. Addicted to pornography? Jesus still loves you. Gay? Jesus still loves you. A habitual liar too terrified to let anyone see the real you? Jesus sees the real you and loves you like crazy.

Everything else you will read in this book—more important, every-thing you encounter in life—should be evaluated with a clear sense of perspective.

Right now your nose might be pressed up against an ugly mishmash of colors and textures that make no sense—and are frightening, to boot. But take a few steps back. You are a work of art. Ephesians 2:10 says, "For we are God's workmanship, created in Christ Jesus to do good works, which God prepared in advance for us to do."

Your life is in the hands of a Master Artist. He has a purpose for your life. Don't ever forget that. Trust in him. Watch as he reveals to you more and more of the Big Picture masterpiece that he wants your life to be. And as you see portions of the painting come together, hold on to that knowledge when you encounter a new section of the canvas of your life—a section that is murky and unfinished, or empty. So empty that it's scary.

Perspective will revolutionize the way you live. So take two giant steps back and use it.

SLICE OF ADVICE:

It's hard to see the Big Picture when your nose is pressed up against it. Actions you take (and decisions you make) in the darkness of confu-sion and despair will likely be mistakes. So don't act, don't conclude, don't decide until you've seen things in the light of God's love. Because only in that light can you see clearly.

DELIVER ON THIS:

Every time you are depressed or face a crisis in your life, before you respond, please go through this exercise. Consider these words from Isaiah 54:10: "'Though the mountains be shaken and the hills be removed, yet my unfailing love for you will not be shaken nor my covenant of peace be removed,' says the Lord, who has compassion on you."

Say this verse out loud, then ask yourself, "In light of the fact that I am adored unconditionally by my Lord, Friend, and Creator, how should I respond to what is happening in my life right now?"

HERE BY CHANCE? NOT A CHANCE!

You've probably heard a teacher utter the cliché, "There's no such thing as a stupid question." Well, actually, there is.

We have asked many stupid questions in our lives, including a few we've posed on purpose. Example one: When getting a tour of a bomber jet at the Air Force Academy, we just had to ask our guide, "Excuse me, Captain, but what junkyard did a whirlwind blow through so that a bunch of spare parts, wires, and scrap metal could accidentally form this complex jet?"

Here's another one, from a tour of the Louvre art museum in Paris. "Excusez-moi, Monsieur Guide de Tours, but how many random spillings of paints did it take before this here *Mona Lisa* was rendered?"

As you might imagine, one of these questions brought us a profanity-peppered tirade and a threat to "tear off your arms and beat you to death with the bloody stumps, you ignorant maggots!"

(The Air Force captain got mad at us too.)

Clearly, the two aforementioned questions were ignorant, even by

Hafer brothers' standards. Intelligent design, such as a bomber jet or masterpiece painting, screams in a big, booming voice, "AN INTELLI-GENT DESIGNER DID THIS, NOT SOME RANDOM BOO-BOO!"

And yet there are people, even some from the scientific community, who claim the universe, including human beings, is merely the product of billions of years of random accidents. This is, if you'll pardon the use of scientific terminology, "a load of horse-puckey."

Just as the vision, passion, and talent of a great painter can be seen in his or her art, God has revealed himself to us through his creation. We should be awed and moved by the intricacy, wonder, and beauty of God's handiwork—the expanse of the sky peppered with stars, the vast-ness of the oceans, the complex marvel that is the human body.

Do you ever really look around and consider how amazing creation is? Do you take time to ponder the beauty of God's handiwork and how awesome he is? Ever thought of the mass of the sun, which, by compar-ison with other stars, is average at best? And it's just one of millions. In fact, in the Bible's account of creation, only a handful of words are devoted to the creation of stars. Much more ink is given to the creation of women and men.

God made *light*. How cool is that? Where did he get the idea for that one? Have you ever truly pondered this? He invented, created, and is busy right now sustaining all of the world, all of life.

Sadly, with the growth of technology—and a few people's egos—we are less and less in awe of God's artistry. We have supposedly figured out so many things that we have forgotten how great God is. Recently, we heard about an association of biology teachers who came to the learned conclusion that the universe came into being without any help from a Supreme Being.

What does all this have to do with you? Simple. If you believe that you and all around you are just the by-products of some cosmic acci-dent, you might live as if this lie were true. If we are all just accidents, merely "ooze that got lucky," then why does life matter at all? What possible meaning could it hold?

Ever wonder why so many people sleepwalk through life, check out of life (via suicide or chemical dependency), or treat other people's lives like a used Kleenex? You might have to look no farther than some college and high school biology texts.

By contrast, knowing the truth—that human beings are beloved works of art, crafted by the almighty God—compels us to check *into* life, do a big, off-the-high-dive cannonball right in the middle of it.

Think about it: Michelangelo toiled on his back for four years, painting the Sistine Chapel's ceiling, carefully rendering the details even in the dark corners because, as he explained to critics who claimed no one would look at those parts of his work, "God will see." Would he have suffered for his art if he thought he was just a hunk of ooze, painting for the amusement of a bunch of other ooze blobs?

Would Mother Teresa have devoted her life to loving and caring for the poor and diseased if she saw them as just a bunch of little accidents rather than God's children?

Would thousands of people (i.e., Jesus Freaks) have sacrificed their lives for their faith if they believed they were just biological accidents, by-products of "lucky ooze," randomly happening upon a cause with no meaning, in an accidental world? Quick, how many nihilist martyrs can you name? How about nihilist humanitarians, then? Okay, time's up. It's time to talk about Bach.

What kind of symphonies would good old J. S. Bach have composed if he signed every sheet of music (all ten thousand of 'em), not with Soli Deo Gloria (To God Alone Be the Glory), but rather with Soli Whatever Gloria? Would he have written music at all?

Like Michelangelo, Mother Teresa, and Bach, God put you here for a purpose. And he is not distant from his creation. He is involved. He cares. You are not just a work of art; you're a work of *heart*. The all-powerful Master Creator of the Universe made you in his image, and he loves you personally. He wants to have a close relationship with you. He wants that so much that he sent his singular Masterpiece, Jesus Christ, to draw you to his side.

SLICE OF ADVICE:

Tonight, go outside and look at the sky. (The Bible says, "The heavens declare the glory of God; the skies proclaim the work of his hands" [Psalm 19:1].) Take some time to stare at the vast canopy above you, the stars, the moon. As you take it all in, commit to living in light of the fact that you were designed by the almighty God, the same one who placed every star in the sky. You're not an accident. You are a marvelous creation, already in the process of sharing your gifts and making your unique impact on your world.

DELIVER ON THIS:

We promise not to ask you to memorize too many verses in this book, but here's one worth tattooing on your brain: "So God created man in His own image; in the image of God He created him; male and female He created them" (Genesis 1:27 NKJV). Remember this one whenever anyone suggests you are an accident. Here's the real deal: When God was knitting you together in your mother's womb, you weren't an accident waiting to happen; you were a miracle waiting to emerge.

WHO'S YOUR FRIEND?

Who is your all-time, number-one best friend? The person you would single out above all the others? Maybe it's someone you've known since elementary school. Maybe it's a teammate or member of your youth group. Or perhaps it's a boyfriend or girlfriend.

Whatever the case, think for a few moments about what makes this friend shine brighter than the others. Do it right now. Take your time; we'll wait for you at the beginning of the next paragraph.

What words and images popped into your mind? What distinguishes a *best* friend from a "good friend" or even a "close friend"? If you are like most people, you and your best friend share common interests. And you probably can name several things that you admire about this person—a sense of humor, intelligence, confidence, and generosity.

When you are together, you probably find that your personalities complement one another. Perhaps your friend's strength in a certain area balances your weakness or lack of experience in that area. More than this, you simply click together. You communicate well, often without uttering a word. And when you do converse, you might find yourselves finishing each other's sentences.

All of the above factors are important in a friendship, but they probably don't get to the core of what gives your best friend the top position in your heart and mind. Think about it for a moment—isn't your best friend the one you *trust* more than the others? The one you can depend on to stand by your side, regardless of circumstances or consequences? The one with whom you can share secret fears or come to for advice on sensitive—even embarrassing—matters? The one you know will care about you no matter what?

There is nothing like a true, faithful friend. And Jesus is that kind of friend to you. You may have thought of Jesus as your creator, your leader, your teacher, and the Lord of your life. And he is all of those things. But Jesus is also your friend. "What a Friend We Have in Jesus" isn't just a hymn sung by old people; it's a rock-solid truth. In the New Testament, Jesus reveals that those who follow him are his friends, not merely disciples or members of some divine posse.

Acknowledging Jesus as your friend can bring a whole new dynamic to your relationship with him.

First, realizing that Jesus is your friend can make your relationship with him closer. Think about it—you may admire a celebrity or famous athlete, or even your favorite recording artist—but how *close* could you become to this person?

It might be a teacher or pastor or coach or boss that you admire. But even here, roles like teacher/student or coach/athlete or employer/employee can block closeness. In fact, many teachers and managers are cautioned against becoming too close to those under their authority.

But it's a different story with friends. You can get as close as you need to with them. Jesus calls you his friend, and there is no professionally mandated distance between the two of you. You can get as close as you want. You can dispense with the rules and formalities and pour out your heart to him. Jesus doesn't offer you the corporately mandated four-second, firm-grip handshake. He'll give you a hug. You can be honest with him. You can cry before him, on him, if you need to. And you don't need to schedule an appointment. As with any true friend, his door is always open.

Secondly, because Jesus is your friend, you can communicate with him about *anything*. With a teacher or boss, you approach them about subjects within their domain of knowledge and scope of influence. You discuss what's "appropriate." You might have a great biology teacher, for example, someone who really knows her way around a mitochondria. But are you going to go to this person for advice on how to get along with your parents?

But a best friend cares about *all* areas of your life. Jesus will listen to your thoughts, opinions, and concerns, regardless of the topic. You can come to him even when you aren't seeking wisdom or guidance. You can approach Jesus merely to tell him how you feel.

At this point, we know that some of you are saying, "Jesus wouldn't want to be friends with someone like me." Don't be so sure. Here's what some of Jesus' contemporaries said about him: "Here is a glutton and a drunkard, a friend of tax collectors and 'sinners'" (Matthew 11:19).

What's more, back in New Testament days, it wasn't just a social faux pas to associate with the likes of boozehounds, prostitutes, and tax collectors; it violated Jewish law.

So, you're a sinner (maybe—*gulp!*—even an aspiring tax collector). Jesus still wants to be your friend. He's been making friends with sinners for thousands of years. He's really good at it.

Okay, now it's time to backtrack and read the first paragraph of this chapter again. We'll wait here for you.

All done? Good. Now, consider this: If God has blessed you with an earthly best friend, you are fortunate indeed. But don't forget that you have a heavenly Best Friend too. And he would love to hear from you. Right now would be fine.

 **SLICE OF ADVICE:**

Courtesy of Thomas Merton (he's old-school, and he's good): "That is His [the Lord's] call to us—simply to be people who are content to live close to Him and to renew the kind of life in which the closeness is felt and experienced."

 **DELIVER ON THIS:**

The next time your best friend—or any friend—gives you a gift or pays you a compliment, remember that your friend Jesus gave you life itself. And he died for your sins so that life doesn't ever have to end. That's what kind of friend Jesus is to you. What kind of friend are you being to him? Right now think of one thing you can do this year to be a better friend to Jesus. After all, friendship is a two-way relationship.

YOUR VERDICT IS IN: NOT GUILTY

A t this point, based on our experience, you are probably in one of two head spaces after getting this far into *Pizza*:

Space #1: You understand the value of your Creator-God's love for you and you realize the importance of viewing your life from that perspective—through the lens of love.

And you believe that Jesus is your friend. In fact, you and he might be longtime buds.

Or you might reside in Space #2: You doubt that God truly loves you. You can understand why he might love "good people" like Steven Curtis Chapman or Joy Williams or Max Lucado. But not someone like you. Not someone who has done the things you've done. Not someone who, if you're truly honest, doesn't really love God. And Jesus as a friend? Not a chance. You can picture Jesus as your judge, your accuser, even your spiritual advisor. But not a true, close friend.

If you are a resident of Space #2, there's a good chance that your old nemesis Guilt put you there. (And even if you are a grateful resident of

Space #1, you might find that someday Guilt will try to relocate you or someone you care about. So please don't skip ahead to the next chapter just yet. We might have something for you.)

We have found two primary barriers, two thick walls that separate God from his people. One is pride (which we'll talk about later). The other is guilt, which we'll talk about right now.

Guilt over what you have done or failed to do makes you feel dirty, small, insignificant, and unworthy of God's love and attention. It's time to shed that guilt like dead snakeskin.

"But you don't know the things I've done," you might be protesting. True, we don't. But consider the following examples that we do know about:

- Paul persecuted Christians, even presided over their brutal murders.
- Peter denied Christ, his friend and master, on the most excruciating night of his life.
- David committed adultery and abused his power in a murderous way. Like an Old Testament Tony Soprano, he put out a hit on an innocent man just to cover up his own sin.
- Samson was a hothead, a horn dog, and a tramp.
- Want a more modern example? Brennan Manning, one of our favorite writers—and perhaps the bravest Christian communicator today—relates that at one tragic point in his life, he broke every one of the Ten Commandments.

But they all found peace. David ended up being called "a man after God's own heart." Peter was eventually killed for standing up for his faith. Paul went on to become one of Christianity's most bold and outspoken crusaders. Think he was plagued and paralyzed by guilt? Consider these words he wrote in Romans 8:1–2: "There is now no condemnation for those who are in Christ Jesus, because through Christ Jesus the law of the Spirit of life set me free from the law of sin and death."

Still think you're too bad a person to have Jesus as your friend and savior? Really? Have you publicly and defiantly denied Christ this past week? Murder any Christians lately? Broken every single commandment? We didn't think so.

Even if you have done something truly terrible, you're in good company. Good, forgiven, loved company.

So it's time to shuck off that guilt. How? Fall into God's forgiving, loving arms. Let your broken self be loved by God. That is what he does best. Say you're sorry. Throw yourself on the mercy of God's court. Want a model on how to do that last one? Check out David's confession in Psalm 51.

If you are still struggling with your not-guilty verdict, please consider your situation from this perspective (there's that P word again): Your sin isn't bigger than God's love and forgiveness. We promise you that. Not the abortion you had, or aided and abetted. Not the sexual experimentation. Not the secret drug habit. Not the Internet porn obsession. Not the cruel streak toward those younger and weaker than you. Not the lying that you can't control.

Jesus, in his broken body, absorbed every wrong thing you have ever done—and ever will do. The sin is no longer yours. He made it his. The Bible goes so far as to say, "He became sin." Then he died, taking all that sin down with him. He was buried, but he rose to life. The sin, however, stayed buried. It's worm food, our friend. You are free of it.

Want another picture? Jesus became dirty to make you clean. He was pure enough, strong enough, tough enough, loving enough to carry all the world's sin. That means yours too. And he's also more than capable of carrying your every loss, disappointment, wound, dark and secret fear.

Want to know what God thinks of you? One of our favorite writers, Max Lucado, says it so well: "God thinks you're wonderful." He can live anywhere and everywhere in the universe and he wants to live in your heart.

God is crazy about you. Crazy. Not fond. Not warmly loving. He strains his eyes searching for you. And when he sees you, even though you are a long way off, he makes a mad sprint down the road for you. Sandals smacking, robe flapping, dust flying. And when he gets to you, he hugs you and smothers you with kisses. He is drunk with joy.

Okay, one more time: Nothing you've done is bigger than God's love. Guilt has no chance against God's crazy, frozen-heart-melting brand of love. Guilt can't take that kind of heat.

 SLICE OF ADVICE:

We've all done terrible things, and it's tempting to get dragged down by our own shame over what we've done. But we shouldn't look at guilt from a flawed human perspective; we should realize that it's God's viewpoint that counts. And here's that viewpoint: "For I will forgive their wickedness and will remember their sins no more" (Hebrews 8:12). As Daniel put it, "The Lord our God is merciful and forgiving, even though we have rebelled against him" (Daniel 9:9).

 DELIVER ON THIS:

The next time you feel guilt forming a barrier between you and God's love, re-read the aforementioned examples of God's forgiveness in action. Check out David's story, Samson's, Jonah's. Throughout history, God has forgiven murderers, traitors, and cowards. He will forgive you too. Also, memorize 1 John 1:9: "If we confess our sins, He is faithful and just to forgive us our sins and to cleanse us from all unrighteousness" (NKJV). Two things about this verse: First, when it says God is "faithful," that means he'll do it every time. Second, note that the verse says "all unrighteousness." When God makes you clean, he doesn't miss those hard-to-reach places in the dark corners of your heart. All means all. Every last shred and scrap.

DO THE DO

We have both worked a bit in the world of advertising. It's an interesting game, often won by who can make up the most convincing lie about a mediocre product. (If you can get a recording artist to sell out and let a once-great song become a commercial jingle, so much the better.) Fortunately, we both had the good sense to get out of our particular corners of the advertising world before they completely sucked our souls dry.

But advertising does have its good side. (We especially like ads for books by a certain gangly writing duo.) We still find ourselves smiling in admiration and approval when some agency really nails a clever ad slogan, something that becomes part of everyday conversation. (And that, predictably, many other ad agencies start copying or co-opting for their stuff.)

One of our favorites is Nike's "Just Do It." It's short. It's simple. It's to the point. But what we like most about it is this: The person or people who came up with these three words understand something about

American culture. We are world-class excuse-makers and procrastinators. Many of us even put off procrastinating until a later date—when we get caught up on all the procrastinating in which we are already behind.

Now, maybe we are preaching to the choir here, because you are at least motivated enough to read this book, but we encourage you to overcome the resistance, boredom, and fear that will rob you of truly living your life. There is a difference between *living* and existing.

Every day we encounter cell-phone-carrying, corporate-jargon-spouting, suit-wearing, soul-less office monkeys who are merely existing. Just putting in time. Living without passion, without purpose. Corpses with pulses. But you might see younger versions of this Parade of the Living Dead in your school, even your church. People with intriguing philosophies emblazoned on their T-shirts or bumper stickers. People who talk big. But when it comes to action, to Just Doing It, they have no game. Their motto should be "Just Talk About It" or "Just Watch Other People Do It—Then Criticize Them."

Don't let this happen to you. We aren't too proud to plead this again, in capital letters this time: DON'T LET THIS HAPPEN TO YOU! Don't become a zombie.

We will bet that your heart is calling you to do something with your life. It might not be something on a grand scale, but it will be significant. That's because it is your unique calling, you one-of-a-kind child of a loving, genius God. (Yeah, that's right, we're talkin' to you.)

Today we hear a lot of platitudes about dreaming big dreams. Freeing your mind. Unleashing your imagination. And these are nice sentiments, but by themselves they are just so much smoke. After all, those corporate zombies we mentioned earlier probably have dreams too (or at least they did before they went to one too many Corporate New-Paradigm Symposiums).

The problem is that an unleashed imagination and a freed mind won't get you anywhere if your buttocks are rooted to the TV-room couch or your eyes are locked on a video game screen. And dreams are cool, but the problem with them is that you usually have to be asleep to have one. Let's get real here. It will take real time, real effort, real sweaty hard work to actually get something done. At some point, you must get out of Dream Mode—and even Planning Mode—and into Action Mode. Inventor Thomas Edison wisely noted that many people miss out on opportunity "because it's dressed in overalls and looks like work."

"Right now" is the only guarantee you have in this life. The Bible wisely warns about bragging, "Tomorrow I'll do this or that." We don't know what tomorrow will bring. Or even if tomorrow will get here.

So don't wait to do a kind deed. To say something loving. To write that poem or psalm or song. To finish that drawing or painting or sculpture. To make that phone call. To say that prayer. To issue that apology. To stop that bad habit (e.g., sin). After all, one of the most dangerous lies in the whole world is "I'll stop that sin—tomorrow."

God has given you abilities. He has given you a light to shine. You might think the little torch you are carrying isn't big enough to make a difference. But if you don't keep that baby lit and hold it high, you deprive the world of some light. Think about that. Don't be a light-robber.

Putting your God-given talents and insights to work is one of the most satisfying things you will ever do. As you do what God created you for, your sense of purpose gets bigger and stronger. And you become closer to the One who gave you those abilities. You, the creation, work hand in hand with the Creator. And few things are as beautiful as that.

The life that energizes, the life that shines, the life that fulfills, is a life of *doing*, not talking about what you're gonna do someday. The Bible warns that faith without works is dead. And dead faith, like road kill, stinks. It's not much to look at either. The meaningful life is a life of action. Go get some.

 ## DOUBLE SLICE OF ADVICE:

1. From Hippocrates (even more old-school than Thomas Merton): "Activity strengthens. Inactivity weakens."

2. "Let us not become weary in doing good, for at the proper time we will reap a harvest if we do not give up" (Galatians 6:9).

 ## DELIVER ON THIS:

Write down the following encouragement from John Wesley (yeah, he's the "Wesley" in Wesleyan Church). Hey, if you have an entire denomination named after you, your words are worth noting. Then, keep the card someplace you'll see it. We're using ours as bookmarks. You'll probably come up with something more creative.

Do all the good you can,
By all the means you can,
In all the ways you can,
In all the places you can,
At all the times you can,
To all the people you can,
As long as ever you can.

YOUR OWN PERSONAL FAIL-SAFE

We are occasionally asked to speak at middle school or high school graduations—usually when the originally scheduled speaker, such as Bobo the Clown: Master of Balloon Animals or Mr. Embree: The Nine-Fingered Former Woodshop Teacher, has cancelled.

We probably won't get to speak at your graduation, but we can still give you the one piece of advice we share with every graduating class desperate enough to welcome one of us as a speaker: "I hope you fail."

We're not kidding. And there's no hidden meaning in those four words up there. We care about you, and we want you to have a happy, fulfilling life. We still hope you fail.

Wait a minute, you might be thinking, *aren't you the two knuckle-heads who, just one chapter ago, encouraged me to be bold, get off my couch, and take action? And now you're saying you hope I fail? May I ask why?*

Yes, you may. And thank you for being so polite about it. You might think that we drop the big F-bomb (F as in Failure, of course) just because we want to be different from all the inspiring graduation speakers who urge their young audiences to "Follow your dreams!" "Reach for the stars!" and "Believe in the power of You!"

Well, yeah, being different from those vapid platitude-mongers is part of the reason. See, lofty clichés like those make us want to hurl. But that's not the only motivation for wishing failure upon today's teens.

We have several other less-reactionary reasons.

First, if you are failing every once in a while, it means you are at least *trying* to do something. You are seeking out challenges, even though those challenges may sometimes beat you like a piñata on Cinco de Mayo.

Second, you can learn a complete *Encyclopedia Britannica*'s worth of knowledge from failure. Yeah, sometimes the lessons are painful. Failure doesn't grade on a curve. Failure doesn't care if you have a note from your mom. Failure doesn't throw out your lowest grade. And this leads to the third reason for our advice. . . .

Failure makes you tough. You've probably heard the stories: Michael Jordan—cut from his high school basketball team. Van Gogh—never had a painting sell until after he died. The Jenkins-LaHaye "Left Behind" series—turned down by almost everyone in Christian publishing before finally finding publication—and about fifty-seven gazillion readers.

Hey, even lesser-known people like us Hafer brothers get to fail. (Lots.) We were once told by someone very powerful in the book industry that we were, and we quote, "unpublishable." That was more than thirty books ago. And believe us, we'd like to tell that critical person, "Who's unpublishable now, you no-taste hack? How'd you like to eat about thirty books' worth of 'unpublishable' material?" But we are far too mature to resort to such childish reactionism.

The point is, whether you are a famous artist, world-class athlete, or lanky mid-level author, rejection can fuel your determination. It can help you realize that very little in life is simply handed to you. You want to accomplish something in life? You'll have to work for it. Speaking of Michael Jordan—and we were just two paragraphs ago—Todd had the chance recently to meet Bill Wennington, Jordan's teammate on some of the NBA championship Chicago Bulls teams. Know what Wennington said about his famous colleague? "Michael Jordan became the greatest basketball player in the history of the game not because of his God-given physical skills, but because of the way he developed those skills. There have been so many superlatives used to describe his work ethic that new words had to be invented."

Jordan wouldn't have developed that work ethic had he not been cut from his team his sophomore year. But the pain of being cut drove him to work on his shots—by the hundreds. It caused him to get up before dawn to make himself the kind of basketball player no coach would ever cut again.

In the Hafer brothers' case, rejection caused us to read everything we could about becoming more effective writers. We took classes. We attended seminars. We sought advice. We wracked our brains for new ideas. And we wrote, rewrote, and re-rewrote. We ran Bic pens dry. We wore Ticonderoga No. 2 pencils down to the size of your little toe. We filled up more yellow legal pads than Johnnie Cochran. In fact, when someone (usually a relative who wants to borrow money) tells us, "You're great writers!" we smile and say, "Not really. But we're pretty decent *re*-writers."

So again, we hope you fail. Not because failure hurts (we wish we could spare you that, but it's part of the deal), but because the hurt helps fuel the drive to succeed. The hurt is a cornerstone of the work ethic that makes success possible. The hurt is part of the education process.

So, from two supposedly unpublishable writers to you: May you know the kind of failure that ultimately leads to success.

 ## DOUBLE SLICE OF ADVICE:

1. "Success is not in never falling, but in rising every time you fall." Confucius
2. "Though a righteous man falls seven times, he rises again" (Proverbs 24:16).

PLEASE, EASY ON THE CHEESE

If you watch enough TV programs or movies, you might get the mistaken idea that failure can be avoided if you *just believe in yourself.* How many times have you heard a movie or TV show end on this particular pile of word poo? With apologies to Reese Witherspoon and every other Hollywood icon who has uttered this cliché, we say, Just Get Real.

Failure is *unavoidable* if you are trying to accomplish anything significant in life. No amount of belief in yourself is going to protect you from falling short once in a while. Besides, shouldn't you be putting your belief in Someone much greater than yourself? We'll let one of our favorite writers, G. K. Chesterton, have the last word on the subject: "The men who really believe in themselves are all in lunatic asylums."

DELIVER ON THIS:

The next time you fail, conduct a Failure Autopsy. Take time to look over what failed, examine it carefully. Plop the various parts of the failure on the scale and look for telltale clues. It might be helpful to bring in a fellow Failure Coroner or two for their expert opinions. Try to decide the following:

1. What caused the failure? Was there a sole cause, or were there multiple factors?
2. Was the cause primarily external or internal?
3. Was the "death" due to natural causes, or was there foul play involved?
4. What can be done to prevent the failure and ensure success the next time—what are the lessons to be learned and applied in the future?

Over time, the Failure Autopsy can become a habit, and you'll get better and better at it. Beware the first time, though. It can be messy and smelly and intimidating and unpleasant. But it has to be done if you want to get at the truth.

KNOW FEAR, NOT "NO FEAR"

We don't see nearly enough written about vomiting in today's books. This chapter is intended to, at least partially, rectify the retching deficit.

In particular, we want to talk about two famous pukers. The first is Henry Fonda. Now, you might know more about Bridget Fonda than her late, great, grandpa Henry. But Henry was a legend of stage and screen. He was an Academy Award winner. He's a Hollywood legend.

But even late in his long, successful career, at age seventy-five, he was blowing his groceries before every stage performance. And this wasn't because of bad backstage catering. He was still afraid, even though he could probably recite his lines in his sleep; still nervous, even after thousands of performances had endeared him to audiences and solidified his position as one of America's all-time great performers.

Another hero of hurling was basketball legend Bill Russell. Russell was *the* man on the Boston Celtics teams that won eleven NBA titles.

He was an absolute beast of a rebounder and shot-blocker. If you watch ESPN Classic, you know what we mean. Russell was a more athletic Shaq O'Neal. (And he could shoot free throws better too.) But even after he had run out of fingers on which to put his NBA championship rings, what was he doing before a big game? You got it—hurling like Henry.

Want one more example of fear—without the nausea references? How about Arthur Ashe, an African-American tennis great who was to his sport what Tiger Woods has been to golf. He revolutionized his sport, becoming the first great male double-A tennis player. Every time this soft-spoken man destroyed an opponent on the court, he helped destroy the myth that tennis was a white man's game—a rich white man's game.

Ashe uttered one of our favorite quotes, especially in this day of bravado-soaked No Fear T-shirts and posters. He said, "You never really conquer the fear of losing. You keep challenging it."

You have the point by now. It is okay to be afraid. Even so afraid you think you might chuck your roast. People who were among the greatest at what they did felt the same way.

And people who aren't even close to being the greatest at anything feel the same way too. Every time we publish a book, fear haunts us. Will anybody buy this book? we wonder. Will critics say nasty things about us? Will our publisher be angry with us if we don't hit sales projections? Will this be the last time we get published?

We face similar fears before we do comedy at a club or corporate gig—or even speak at a church. In fact, we'd probably call on "Ralph O'Rourke," just like Russell and Fonda, if the specter of public speaking didn't make us so nervous that we can't eat for many hours before standing in front of an audience.

So if fear haunts you as you seek to achieve your life goals, you are not alone. Many others feel the same way. And those cocky dudes with their pasted-on sneers and No Fear gear are probably just too scared to admit the truth about how they feel. Ironic, isn't it?

Here is something you might not have seen in a book before—especially one from a Christian publisher: Fear can be your friend. Fear heightens your senses. Fear lets you know that you are involved in something that matters. Fear pushes you to pray, because you know that the challenge at hand is something for which you need God at your side.

Former Los Angeles Laker great Magic Johnson is one of our all-time favorite basketball players. Some say he is the best ever. But even Magic couldn't make fear disappear. He said that he feared, truly feared, Larry Bird of the Boston Celtics. But at the same time, Magic relished competing against Bird. Why? Because Bird always brought out the best in him. And when his team defeated Bird's, especially in the NBA finals, the victory was honey-sweet because he knew that he had accomplished something great.

The bottom line: Don't be afraid of fear. It just might be life's way of telling you, "Okay, it's on." The key is to make sure that fear sparks action, not inaction. Don't let it keep you from doing the good work that God has planned for you to do. There will never be a moment in your life when you don't have the power to do that work—or at least lay the foundation for it. So face fear. Welcome it as a friend. But not such a good friend that you're unwilling to puke on its shoes.

 **SLICE OF ADVICE:**

"Make the most of every opportunity you have for doing good" (Ephesians 5:16 TLB).

DELIVER ON THIS:

Next time you're afraid—before a final exam, before a big game, before a solo in church, whatever—don't cower in the face of that fear. Acknowledge it. Accept it. Feed off of it. Look at fear as your classic rival, your Larry Bird. The one who is going to make you bring your A-game. Talk to God. Tell him how you feel. Ask him to help fear bring out the best in you—to heighten your senses, sharpen your abilities, and fortify your resolve. Then get out there and try to take fear to school. It won't be easy, but keep trying. Because if you can learn to go toe-to-toe with fear, you're going to get very good at what you do. Scary-good.

TIME TO REHEAT IT

Thanks for sharing *Pizza* with us to this point. If this book were a twelve-slice pie, you'd have devoured more than two slices already. We hope you're not full yet, because there's a lot of tasty stuff to come. (Hey, we haven't talked about sex, drugs, media violence, or Internet porn yet. We're just getting warmed up.)

But before we get to that stuff, we need to take a break and review a few key truths from the first seven chapters. What we have given you so far is foundational for understanding and applying what is to come, so give these thoughts a few spins on the microwave turntable of your brain.

1. Perspective is key to an effective, happy life. You need to approach life from the following perspective: You are a masterpiece child of God, and he loves you like crazy. You are no accident. Think of this truth as a pair of prescription

sunglasses that helps you see the important things in life with high-definition clarity—and filter out the annoying glare that would otherwise obscure your view.

2. Jesus is your friend—such a good friend that he put his life on the line for you. There is nothing you can't tell him. And there is nothing you can do to make him stop loving you. Some say Jesus is hopelessly in love with his people. We get what they're trying to say, but we think they have it wrong. The truth is, Jesus is *hopefully*, not hopelessly, in love with you.

3. Because of Jesus' sacrifice, God can make you completely guilt-free and clean from sin. Divine forgiveness is freely available to anyone willing to accept it. The Bible is filled with a bunch of cowards, murderers, and infidels that make the dudes on *America's Most Wanted* look like American Girl dolls. But every last one of them got clean, thanks to God's industrial-strength grace.

4. All of the truths above should motivate you to live a life of action. Do something with your life. Don't be a color commentator on life; get in the game. You've got game; we know you do. Bring it. Show it.

5. Failure is inevitable if you want to accomplish anything in life. But that's okay. Because failure can make you tough, make you smart, and make you determined.

6. Fear is nothing to be afraid of. Fear can become your classic rival, the one who always brings out your A-game.

THE VIRGIN INTERVIEWS

Here's the deal: This chapter is about sex. We were tempted to fill these pages with scary stats about date rape and sexually transmitted diseases and unwanted pregnancies—and warnings of how sexual impurity can break the hearts of your parents, friends, and youth leaders.

Then we thought it might be better if we could simply share with you the thoughts of some real, live virgins. Virgins aren't an endangered species, despite the impression you might get from watching TV shows like *The O. C.*—or *Jerry Springer.*

So we sat down with three virgins we know. (And in case you're wondering, no, they're not ugly. Far from it.) We had questions. They had answers.

Q: *Is it really difficult to be a virgin in today's world?*
Vickie: Sometimes. I mean, sex is everywhere. Music videos, TV shows, movies. It's a major topic of conversation at school too. And it's not just guys who talk about it. So it's not like you can

avoid thinking about it. It's in your face practically every day. You get thoughts in your head. You get feelings. The question is, what are you going to do—or not do—about them?

Q: *Would most Christian adults be surprised if they knew how many Christian teens are sexually active?*

Andi: Probably. But they might also be surprised at how many non-Christians are abstaining for one reason or another. A lot of them say they just aren't ready.

Q: *"Ready," that's a rather vague term. . . .*

Andi: Exactly. Don't get me wrong—any reason that keeps people pure is okay with me. But how do you know when you're "ready"? I mean, we're talking about sexual and spiritual intimacy here, not cooking hamburgers. You can't make such an important, irrevocable decision based on whether you feel ready. You might feel ready one day, but a week later you could feel different. Only then it will be too late.

Q: *When you're pressured, either by your friends or a guy, how do you deal with it?*

Laura: The key is to have already made a commitment, in your mind and in your heart. You have to be prepared beforehand. Otherwise you can get caught up in the pressure, or the passion, of the moment. So you make a pact with God. You make a promise to yourself. Some people I know have made a pact with a parent or with a group of friends. I think that's great. Whatever you do, you keep yourself accountable. Because temptation will come, and that purity promise you made might be the only thing that keeps you strong. Because sex is one of the strongest temptations there is. I have committed to staying a virgin until I am married. It's important to me. It's important to God. And I know it will be important to the guy I marry someday. I know he will be relieved, thankful, and appreciative that I took a stand.

Q: *It will be nice going into marriage with no sexual baggage?*

Laura: Sure it will. I don't want to drag a bunch of guilt, bad experiences, secrets, fears about STDs, any of that mess, into the bedroom I'll share with my husband someday.

Q: *A lot of people say that biblically based views on sexuality are out of date, unrealistic. What's your response to that?*

Vickie: Truth never goes out of style, dudes. People forget that God invented sex. Not *Playboy*. Not "Skinemax" or any other cable TV channel. I think God wants his people to have great sex—at the right time and in the right setting. I am trusting God on this one, and I believe he will reward me for staying pure.

Q: *Some of the people who will read this book are—or have been—sexually active. Is it too late for them?*

Andi: No way. Hey, just because you've stepped in dog crap once, that's no excuse to keep doing it. Make a commitment. Turn your life around. Quit playing sexual roulette. Your health, your self-respect, and your relationship with God and all those who love you are at stake here. A girl friend of mine is working on something called "Secondary Virginity." She's putting her past behind her, asking forgiveness, and committing to being pure from here on. I know that the guy she marries someday will appreciate the fight she's putting up now.

Q: *What can adults do for teens like you?*

Andi: Don't pretend sex doesn't exist or that "good" Christians aren't tempted by it. Talk about it. Don't avoid the subject. Don't freak out and turn red if someone mentions the word "penis." Ask questions. Answer questions—honestly. Don't be naïve. Set boundaries. And pray for us. Every day. Because being a virgin can be really, really difficult.

 **SLICE OF ADVICE:**

"But among you there must not be even a hint of sexual immorality, or any kind of impurity . . . because these are improper for God's holy people" (Ephesians 5:3).

PLEASE, EASY ON THE CHEESE

We saw a sexuality "expert" on TV the other day, woofing about how monogamy and sexual purity were contrary to the "natural order" of things. She noted that most animals have multiple sexual partners and have sex whenever they feel like it. To this we retort, "*Good* point, Ms. Sexpert! But hey, our dogs roll in garbage and drink out of the toilet. Monkeys eat their own monkey-doo. Tigers eat their young. So maybe it's not the best idea for human beings, made in God's image, to take their behavioral cues from chimps, dogs, or even wombats.

"One more thing, Ms. Sexpert—we want to test you to see if you really believe that what's good enough for lower mammals is good enough for human beings. So if you come to one of our houses for a visit, let's see if you want to drink out of the toilet. We'll leave the lid up for you."

 **DELIVER ON THIS:**

If you haven't done so yet, make a commitment, right now, to maintain—or reclaim—your sexual purity until you are married. Make a pact with a parent, friend, or youth leader. Make a pact with God. If you want, you can even make your pact with us. E-mail us at *www.haferbros.com,* and we promise to pray for you every day in your battle for sexual purity.

INTERVIEW WITH DRUG-FREE DOUG

We enjoyed our virgin interview so much that we thought we'd take the same approach to this chapter on drugs. It took a little bit longer to find someone who had been completely drug free, especially since we wanted to interview a guy this time. (Never let it be said we aren't all about gender equality.)

Eventually we found a guy we'll call Drug-Free Doug. Here's what we learned from him.

Q: *So you've really never taken an illegal drug? Ever?*
A: Never. Not one snort, one puff, one huff, or one hit.
Q: *What has been the key to your staying drug free?*
A: I'd like to say it was all the anti-drug programs and lectures at school or church—I'm sure they help a lot of people. But in my case, it was more a one-to-one commitment between God and me. I see my mind as a gift from God. I am not saying I am a genius or anything, because I'm not. But my brain is the best thing I have going for me. So I'm not going to ruin it—either

little by little or one giant overdose—with drugs.

Q: Have you been pressured?

A: Absolutely. I don't go around wearing an *I'm Drug Free* T-shirt, but I don't hide my commitment either. So when some people hear about my stand, they do all they can to get me high— trickery, intimidation, bribery, you name it.

Q: Does the pressure ever get to you?

A: Only in that it's annoying. But it's not like it's going to make me weaken. I tell people all the time, "This is my body, my brain." This is what God gave me. I'm not going to dishonor him by using myself as a toxic waste dump. My true friends understand that. When they offer me something, I say, "I don't need that to have a good time." They know that, for me, that's the truth, and they respect it. That's kind of my mantra, you know, when anyone offers me drugs or beer or whatever: "I don't need it."

Q: Aren't you ever curious about what it feels like to be high? Don't you feel like you're missing something?

A: Sure, I might get curious from time to time. But I'm curious about what it feels like to get struck by lightning too. That doesn't mean I'm going to stand on a hill with a nine-iron during an electrical storm.

Q: Why do you think so many of your peers are into drugs?

A: A lot of reasons: boredom, curiosity, a way to deal with pain in their lives. And drug use is quite a trap. Drugs affect your brain, the very organ that you use to determine what is good for you and what isn't. So the more you get high, the more your drug-clouded brain tells you it's okay, and the hole you dig just keeps getting deeper. I can see why people get hopelessly addicted. They think they are doing drugs. In reality, the drugs are doing *them*.

Q: How do you feel about legalizing drugs?

A: Well, let's see, alcohol and cigarettes are legal, and they really enhance the quality of life, don't they? The stories I could tell you about my friends who live with an alcoholic dad or a mom addicted to downers . . .

Q: *But isn't it hypocritical for society to ban certain drugs when substances that are arguably more harmful than marijuana, for example, are perfectly legal? After all, cigarette-related illnesses kill more Americans each year than alcohol, auto accidents, homicide, suicide, AIDS, and illegal drugs combined.*

A: Sure, it's hypocritical, but so what? Giving yourself lung cancer via cigarettes is legal. Clogging your arteries with fatty food is legal. Pickling your liver with alcohol is legal. But I don't see why we should give people yet more legal ways to ruin their lives and the lives of others.

Q: *But what do you say to the people who say it is an individual's right to put whatever he or she wants into the ol' body—or the young body, for that matter?*

A: To a point, I agree with those people. The problem is that when you put drugs into your body, you end up affecting more than just yourself. For example, we already have enough drunk people on the roads—do we need to add coked-out and stoned people too? I'm worried enough about driving the streets as it is.

Q: Some teens we talk to say drugs truly help them cope with life. If not for drugs, they say, they would resort to social isolation, or maybe even violence or suicide.

A: That kind of excuse is weak. Drugs don't help you cope. They destroy your ability to cope. They make you weaker and weaker. More dependent. Dependent on an illusion that the world is something that it's not—and that the user is something that he's not—namely, smart, cool, funny, truly happy, or in control.

I wish some people I knew would just admit the truth: That the only time they're happy is when their brains are so clouded that their perceptions and perspective are warped. It's like saying the only time you can really see yourself clearly is in some bizarre House of Mirrors at a carnival. My friends who use drugs are basically trying to escape from who they are—or make themselves something they are not. But eventually you have to come down, you have to get level, and face the real you.

Q: *What do you think about the people who say God is a crutch, just like substance abuse?*

A: I'd say, "You must be on drugs!" That's just more weak rhetoric. Here's what's real: God helps me deal with real-life problems via real-life solutions. To me, a person on drugs is like a little kid who is scared of something, so he closes his eyes, buries his head under the covers, and pretends the source of the fear doesn't exist. God, on the other hand, gives you the strength and courage to open your eyes and confront the problem.

SLICE OF ADVICE:

We were tempted here to provide advice from the Surgeon General or a doctor friend of ours. But we decided to opt for another first in Christian publishing. We're going to quote Brian Warner—you probably know him as lead singer for the group Marilyn Manson—in a positive light. This is a guy who is on record as a drug user, but in one of his songs ("Coma White"), he's still honest enough to say, "A pill to make you numb / A pill to make you dumb / A pill to make you anybody else. All the drugs in this world won't save her from herself."

DELIVER ON THIS:

Remember that Sexual Purity Pact from the previous chapter? You can do the same thing on the drug front. Your body and your brain are gifts from God. They are the instruments through which you can achieve his purpose for your life. Don't pollute God's gift to you. If you are drug free, don't sacrifice your freedom. If you're using drugs, we aren't going to be so naïve as to tell you to "Just say no" and everything will be fine. It's quite likely that you will need help to get yourself clean. Talk to an adult you can trust to help you find the resources you need. And, please, do it right now. Don't waste one more day of your life being wasted.

A KILLER BOD— NOT WORTH DYING FOR

You probably see them everywhere you go: the mall, the pool, the multiplex—just about every place but the library. "They" are the hardbody hotties. The genetic marvels who have been blessed with toned muscles, perfect skin, and digestive systems that apparently burn fat the way a Porsche Turbo Carrera burns fuel.

And when you can't see these physical wonders in person, they still haunt you, smiling at you—and flexing for you—on TV, on magazine covers, and giant billboards. It's intimidating. Sometimes it's downright depressing.

Guys wish, "Why can't I get my abs to pop like that dude's? And look at those arms—they're bigger than my legs!"

Girls wonder, "Could I *ever* starve myself enough to get as thin as that woman? And it should be against the law to have legs that long and smooth!"

You may ponder how you can compete with all the buff bods, without getting "all swole" yourself. How can you get a date, even get noticed, in the sea of bulging biceps, long legs, and perfect pectorals?

Relax. (Guys: That means stop flexing, okay? You don't need to impress anybody right now, and you're gonna get a cramp if you don't chill. And girls: No need to keep sucking in your gut; you're among friends now.) Before you buy some expensive piece of exercise equipment from a shop-at-home channel or blow hundreds of dollars on questionable herbal supplements, you need to consider a few facts.

First, those magazine supermodels and media stars you envy aren't as perfect as they look. Posters and photos are retouched, airbrushed, and manipulated in all sorts of ways. Even CD cover shots of Christian recording artists are touched up. Blemishes and wrinkles are removed. (For that matter, *pores* are removed!) Flabby arms are made trim; weenie arms are bulked up. And check this—makeup is used to make guys look like they have washboard abs when in reality they don't.

And the oils. Let's not forget the oils that are applied liberally to highlight every sinew, every vein. Sure, you might want to hug these gleaming bods, but they'd probably squirt right out of your arms. (One quick warning to some of you—and you know who you are: Don't get any ideas about this oil thing. Don't sneak into the kitchen and try to Wesson up your biceps or your abs; you're just going to make a mess, stain your clothes, and waste good money. Besides, someone in your house needs that oil for cooking.)

Even the people who do look pretty great without all the gimmicks often get their shine on at a high personal cost. For example, yes, steroids pump you up, but they also might alter your personality—and not in a good way. They can make you short-tempered and violent. They can make you sterile or even kill you. And don't think that the technically legal supplements (like some of those magic "fat incinerators") are necessarily safer. They have killed teens. And that's not a rumor; it's a documented fact. You've probably seen some of the news stories. Just because you can find something on the shelves of your local nutrition store and professional wrestlers endorse it doesn't mean it's safe for you to ingest. Getting a killer bod isn't worth killing yourself, is it?

Granted, having a hottie body might get you noticed by members of the opposite sex. But if you want an actual relationship, you must have something more to offer than delicious deltoids and oh-my-goodness obliques. After all, gorillas are powerful and physically intimidating, but you don't see them getting lots of dates, do you? (Unless it's with other gorillas.)

Once you've captured someone's attention, you're going to need to keep that attention if you want to have a meaningful relationship. You need more than sinew, teeth, and hair. You need a heart that cares, a mind that thinks and wonders, a soul that reflects God's light. When someone asks your boyfriend or girlfriend what is that magic "something" that sparked the romance between the two of you, do you really want the answer to be, "Well, more than anything else, it was the 5 percent body fat!"

There's nothing wrong, of course, with wanting to be fit. Your body is a temple after all, not a Porta Potti. A balanced diet is a good idea, but a celery stick in each hand is not a balanced meal. The same principle applies to a couple of protein shakes.

A sensible workout program is a good idea too. But do it for the right reasons. Do it to be healthy, not to be a date magnet. If you want to improve your fitness level, check with a doctor—especially about herbal supplements and their pros and cons. (In other words, don't buy your supps from that hairy guy named Fabiano who wears lots of gold chains and hangs out by the drinking fountain at the gym.)

Finally, keep your fitness goals in perspective. Don't become obsessed with your body image at the expense of your friendships, your schoolwork, or your spiritual life. After all, someday your muscles are going to lose some of their size and tone, no matter how hard you try to prevent it. But if you live right, your relationships, your mind, and your soul can keep right on growing.

One final thought here: Someday your earthly body will be reduced to ashes in a crematorium or drained of all its vital fluids, pumped full of preservatives, and packed into a coffin. Your soul, on the other hand, is eternal. Think about it—the same soul that is inside you right now, maybe even stirring as you read these words, is the soul that will endure forever. So what do you think you should spend most of your time building?

SLICE OF ADVICE:

"For physical training is of some value, but godliness has value for all things, holding promise for both the present life and the life to come" (1 Timothy 4:8).

DELIVER ON THIS:

Every morning, when you look in the mirror to check your outward appearance, do a "soul check" too. Scrutinize what's on your conscience, what's in your heart. Then decide what the major focus of your day will be: the hair and the skin . . . or the person within?

THE UGLY TRUTH ABOUT PHYSICAL BEAUTY

There is more to attractiveness than the kind of buff body people strive for via hours in the gym, fad diets, and various dietary supplements (the stuff we discussed in the previous chapter).

After all, no one has invented weight lifting or aerobics for the face (at least not yet). And as for the rest of the body, sometimes all the push-ups and pills and Pilates in the world aren't enough to help people in that all-consuming quest for physical beauty. Sometimes you need a little help from your friends Mr. Scalpel, Ms. Needle, and Lady Liposuction.

Several intriguing TV shows are generating much debate as we write this book. At first, Hollywood was obsessed only with remodeling people's houses—and occasionally "pimping their rides." But that wasn't enough. Soon, those wacky TV wizards began to focus their attention to remodeling *people*. Now, shows like *The Swan* and *I Want a Famous Face* might be cancelled by the time this *Pizza* is delivered, but the ugly truths they have revealed about America's obsession with physical beauty will remain.

You know the premise of shows like these: TV producers troll for unhappy people, the bait being the promise of true happiness—courtesy of surgically supplied beauty, a wardrobe makeover, a mouthful of dental work, and the best in hair and makeup products and services.

Chins are chiseled, noses nipped, tummies tucked. Teeth are whitened and straightened. Fat is sucked away. (And this isn't the only thing about these shows that sucks.)

On *The Swan,* which features women, once the newly beautified brides of the TV Frankensteins have undergone their transformations, they are paraded before a panel of judges in a pageant, whose purpose, apparently, is to determine whose artificial beauty looks the most authentic. It's one of the most bizarre things we have ever seen. It's a Darwinian theater of cruelty and vanity that makes us long for the days when "Reality TV" was mostly home videos of guys getting whacked in the junk by their toddlers' plastic baseball bats.

Don't get us wrong. We are not saying people shouldn't bathe or floss or practice good grooming as they try to look their best. We aren't saying people shouldn't diet. And we aren't opponents of plastic surgery. We just ask that you show more maturity than the alleged adults who produce and appear on *Swan*-like shows. We urge you to keep a sense of perspective and balance in your life. Contrast the time you spend reading health, beauty, and fitness articles with the time you spend reading the Bible or other books that feed and renew your spirit.

You pay monthly dues at a gym? Cool, so do we. But do you also give regularly to your church or support a charitable ministry like Compassion International or Feed the Children?

You saving up for a cosmetic procedure of some sort or planning to go on a diet program? That's not necessarily a bad thing. But have you thoughtfully and prayerfully considered if this is the best use of your money? And is all of your saving directed toward this goal? What about a college fund? What about a missions trip? What about a large, one-time gift to a cause you believe in?

God doesn't want to transform your skin. He wants to transform your heart. Here's an ugly truth about outward attractiveness: You can have your skin tucked, sucked, and plucked all you want. It's still going to wrinkle and crinkle someday. Then it is going to die. Your heart, your soul, however, will live forever. And that's why God wants to make them beautiful. For free.

So let God transform the part of you that endures for eternity. And don't worry—you won't have to compete in a Soul Beauty Pageant with anyone, because God sees the unique beauty of every living soul. That's why he's a great God but would be a lousy Reality-TV producer—he wants everyone to win.

 **DOUBLE SLICE OF ADVICE:**

1. "Therefore I tell you, do not worry about . . . what you will eat or drink; or about your body, what you will wear. Is not life more important than food?" (Matthew 6:25).
2. "The Lord does not look at the things man looks at. Man looks at the outward appearance, but the Lord looks at the heart" (1 Samuel 16:7).

PLEASE, EASY ON THE CHEESE

Hollywood is absolutely obsessed with external beauty. Trips to the waxing salon, Botox clinic, and plastic surgeon are as routine as trips to the grocery store. Celebrity magazines are replete with the latest trend in facials, manicures, pedicures, nips, and microdermabrasions. Celebrities seem obsessed with having every part of their anatomy as perfect as possible. We're sure it won't be long before they are lining up to Botox their buttocks. All because they don't want to commit the singular unpardonable show-biz sin: looking bad on camera.

Woe to the celeb who shows up at the Academy Awards actually looking his age, or the hapless starlet who gets sniped by a tabloid photographer while exhaling on the beach.

We want to comment on all of this, but we defer to Robert Redford, who at one time was *the* Hollywood sex symbol. Now approaching age seventy, here's what he said about Hollywood's obsession with surgically supplied temporary beauty: "I'm not afraid [to appear older] because I *am*. It happens to all of us. Some people try to arrest it with cosmetic surgery. I don't happen to be one of those people. I believe you wear your life the way it has been."

He adds that every time you have cosmetic surgery, you, and we quote, "lose a piece of your soul."

Well said, Robert. Maybe that explains why so many of the celebrities we've seen interviewed lately seem to have little or no soul at all.

 DELIVER ON THIS:

Every time you spend money or time on your physical appearance, commit to a parallel effort to enhance your inner beauty. For example, after you finish that chapter in your hot new diet book, read a chapter from a Christian book or the Bible. Or after you've finished your morning "attractiveness routine," spend some time praying, addressing any inner blemishes or flaws.

INTERVIEW WITH THE NON-VIRGIN

Never let it be said that the Hafer brothers don't believe in giving equal time. A while after we did our "Virgin Interview," we decided we needed to get a perspective from the other side of the chastity line. We found this guy who isn't a virgin. Not even close to being a virgin. He said some things we expected—and offered several surprise answers as well. . . .

Q: *Do you regret not saving sex for marriage? Be honest.*

A: I do regret it, most of the time. I admit that when I first became sexually active, along with the guilt, there were times I felt cool, experienced. Like I had completed some rite of passage. At times, I actually looked down on my Christian friends who were still virgins. I felt a twisted sense of pride that I was more "worldly" than they were. I can't believe my sensibilities got so warped.

Q: *Warped? How so?*

A: Well, when I stopped feeling like a big playa and took the time to think about what I had given up, I realized two key things:

1. Sin—including sexual sin—breaks God's heart. I was so busy thinking about myself that I lost sight of how what I do affects my Heavenly Father, who loves me. Similarly, I know that what I did disappointed my Christian friends. And if my parents ever find out (and they probably will someday), it will break their hearts too.

2. God invented sex for his people to enjoy. And he knows and understands best the conditions under which sex will be most fulfilling. When I violated his standards for sex, I robbed myself, and others, of the kind of experience they were meant to have. It's amazing the damage we do to ourselves—and the joy we miss—when we think we know better than God.

Q: *How will your sexual past affect your marriage?*
A: I don't like thinking about it. The girl I marry and I won't have the beautiful experience of discovering something brand-new and wonderful together. There will be really difficult questions I will have to answer, and those answers will deeply hurt the person I love most in the world.

Q: *We have to ask: If you had it to do all over again . . .*
A: I'm not sure I can give you the exact answer you want here. I'm just gonna be honest. I should not have made the mistakes I made. I should have obeyed God and waited. I don't always feel terrible about what I did, though. It might make a more compelling case if I did, but, again, there's that honesty thing.

　　What I can say is that how I feel about my sexual past isn't the key. It's how God feels about it that counts. I know that the Bible talks about my body being God's temple. When I think about that concept, it drives home the point for me. I disobeyed God and cheapened myself by doing what I did. That is wrong—no matter how I feel.

Q: *If you get married someday, what will you tell your wife?*
A: The truth.

Q: *Any truth you'd like to tell our readers right now?*
A: Yeah, a few actually. First, having sex doesn't make you an adult or a more sophisticated person. Some of the most imma-

ture, shallow, greedy people I know are sexually active rabbits. Second, yeah, sex before you're married might be fun. (It might also be empty, or unfulfilling, or downright awful.) But even at its best, no amount of fun is worth breaking God's heart. And no amount of fun is worth the risk of pregnancy, STDs, shame, or any of the other stuff that the TV shows, movies, and music videos *don't* tell you about.

The bottom line is that I should have waited. I've had a lot of grief, fear, heartbreak, and problems because I didn't, and I know that there is still more trouble to come. I know I wouldn't be dealing with even a fraction of these problems if I were still a virgin.

 ## SLICE OF ADVICE:

"Flee from sexual immorality . . . he who sins sexually sins against his own body. Do you not know that your body is a temple of the Holy Spirit, who is in you, whom you have received from God? You are not your own; you were bought at a price. Therefore, honor God with your body" (1 Corinthians 6:18–20).

 ## DELIVER ON THIS:

Now that you have finished this chapter, go back to The Virgin Interviews chapter and read it. Then, bound ahead to page 145 and check out the chapter titled "Virgins Revisited." Contrast the consequences—and feelings about those consequences—of the people who stayed pure with those of the one who didn't.

FLASH FORWARD TO YOUR FUTURE

We have both been to a high school reunion or two. (And this doesn't make us uncool. It just makes us older than you. Stuff like needing knee braces to play basketball and driving mini-vans with stuffed Garfields suction-cupped to the rear windows—*that's* what makes us uncool.)

Anyway, we know that most of you reading this book are eons away from a high school reunion, and the subject probably doesn't interest you. That's okay. It doesn't interest us much either—although it is fun to see chubby older guys trying to do the Electric Slide without ripping out the seats of their too-tight Dockers or messing up their comb-overs.

But we did learn a few things at these reunions—things that might help you keep your life right now in perspective. Imagine yourself ten, fifteen, or twenty years in the future. You're sucking in your gut and ready to walk into the ballroom of some Ramada Inn to see many of your old friends—and rivals—for the first time in years.

Here's what you're likely to discover. . . .

1. Some people age like fine wine (or, if you're a Baptist, fine cheese). Others age like a carton of milk that fell out of the grocery bag and slid under the backseat of the minivan, where it remained all summer. (And, no, this isn't a hypothetical example.) Look around you next time you're among classmates. In a few years, many of today's hotties will be "notties." And some of the people who aren't exactly Abercrombie & Fitch models today will turn out to be fit, sharp-looking adults. So don't get obsessed with outward appearance. No matter how good—or bad—you think the skin you're in looks right now, it's temporary. Your soul, on the other hand, is eternal. (Yeah, we've said this before, but it bears repeating.) So what should you spend your time working on?

2. The guy or girl who is filling up the trophy case and athletic records books today might be filling the salad bowl at the Big Country Buffet in a few years. We have both gone to school with amazing athletes, marvelous musicians, and thrilling thespians. Unfortunately, many of them never realized success beyond the walls of high school. Why? Because they failed to grasp that graduation is followed by a little thing called The Rest of Your Life. And those who plan to ride the wave of high school fame and fortune into the future better be prepared for a short ride—with an abrupt ending.

3. Some of the stuff you think is crucial right now will end up being trivial. You might think that high school reunions are all about reliving the Big Game or reminiscing about how hot Valerie the Vixen looked in her homecoming dress. But we were surprised at how *little* story-swapping time was devoted to athletic achievement or grade-point averages or awards won. In fact, when sports came up, the conversation usually veered to something funny or unusual—like the time a certain track runner who shall go unnamed (but his name rhymes with "odd") whipped off his sweats before a big race—and his shorts went right along with them.

4. True friendships endure. Look around you the next time you're in class or at youth group. Look at your friends. We

have found that our best buds from high school are still among our best friends today. There's just something about the people who are by your side when you endure puberty—and chemistry class. The lesson here? We're not saying you shouldn't strive for success in the classroom and extracurricular activities, just don't do it at the expense of your friendships. In ten or twenty years you might not remember your GPA or free-throw percentage, but you will remember your true friends.

 **SLICE OF ADVICE:**

"Do not store up for yourselves treasure on earth, where moth and rust destroy, and where thieves break in and steal. . . . For where your treasure is, there your heart will be also" (Matthew 6:19–21).

 **DELIVER ON THIS:**

The next time you are stressed about something school-related, ask yourself a question like this: In a year—in five years—will this really matter? This exercise will help put things in perspective (that word again). Don't do this as an excuse to blow off a test or fail to learn a part in a school play; do it to determine how much stress, anxiety, and sleeplessness is really warranted in a given situation. You can learn to live with a less-than-stellar grade on a World History pop quiz, but the way you break up with a boyfriend or girlfriend—or how you confront a peer about a drinking or drug problem? That's the kind of thing that will have an enduring impact.

TIME TO REHEAT IT

Cool—you've made it through sex, drugs, and body image—and seen a glimpse of your future as well. We covered some key stuff in this section, and it's time for another review. Here comes the remix. . . .

1. Your body is a gift from God. Use it to honor him. Respect yourself. Keep yourself pure from sexual immorality and drugs.

2. God wants you to have great sex—just not right now. (Unless you're married.)

3. Be careful about obsessing over the skin you're in, at the expense of the real person within the skin. Don't risk your health and sense of true self-worth in a quest for artificial, external beauty.

4. Ten years from now, your list of high school achievements won't matter much, if at all. What will matter is that you were a true, giving, loyal friend who was important in the lives of your homeys.

WAY TO HANG TOUGH

Consider this chapter a pat on your back. You may be like some of the teens we meet across the country; you have kept yourself pure from drugs, sex, pornography, and the like. You have stood up to temptation and pressure, even when it's made you feel like an outcast. We are proud of you.

Or you might be part of another group we have encountered. You have messed up in one or two areas, but stayed strong in others. You are not alone. We know lots of teens who are dabbling in pornography but have resisted the temptation to become sexually active. Others have problems with things like rebellion or a violent temper but have never taken an illegal drug. If this sounds like you, we are proud of you too. Not because one or two areas of your life are a mess, but because you are stiff-arming temptation in others. You haven't waved the white flag and given up on your whole life. Stay strong. And go reclaim that lost territory.

Finally, you might be like a few of the kids that Jedd works with every day. You might really have to wrack your brain to think of one destructive thing you haven't already done. Believe it or not, this chapter is for you too, because it's not too late for you. It's not too late to stop playing Russian roulette with your body, your mind, and your soul. It's not too late to ask for forgiveness and turn your life around. To paraphrase our friends in Superchic(k), don't let life just happen to you. You, happen to life!

Whatever your situation, we encourage you to stay pure, or get pure. And not just because we don't want you suffering with an STD, burned out on drugs, in jail, or dead.

Here's something you might not have thought of before: Abstinence is good practice for the rest of your life. For example, you might think that once you get married all of that sexual self-control you developed gets tossed out the window. Nope.

You will need to control your sexual urges when you are married, just as you need to control them now. You might end up with a job that puts you on the road much of the time, and believe us, the road is littered with temptation.

Or your spouse might suffer from an illness or injury that precludes him or her from having sex—perhaps for a long time. It happens, more often than you think. When it does, you will be grateful for the self-control muscles you can build right now.

Many adults have pitifully weak ab (as in "abstinence") muscles. A *Newsweek* cover story noted that 50 percent of men and 35 percent of women had been unfaithful to their spouses. And in today's materialistic age, it's interesting to note that 50 percent of Porsche owners and 46 percent of BMW owners confessed to being unfaithful to their spouses. You can be stronger than they are. Your generation can show today's adult generation how it's supposed to be done. So build those abs.

The same principle applies to drinking. Life doesn't turn into one big Smirnoff Ice or Budweiser commercial once you hit the legal drinking age. You might decide, as many Christians do, that alcohol isn't for you. But it will be readily available, and, just like now, you will be bombarded with advertisements telling you that life will be a rockin' party and you'll be surrounded by your drinking buddies—and hot members of the opposite sex—if you drink the right brand of fermented beverage. It's one thing to resist alcohol when it's illegal for you. It's another matter when it's legal and encouraged. Again, it all comes back to self-control.

If you hit twenty-one and feel drinking is appropriate for you, the principle still works. If you decide to drink, you will need to, as those aforementioned ads tell you in tiny type or a soft, almost subliminal voice, *"Drink responsibly."* You will need to control *when* you drink and *how much* you drink.

If you get behind the wheel of a two-thousand-pound vehicle while intoxicated, you are putting your life at risk—as well as the lives of innocent people who are sharing the road with you.

Additionally, according to *USA Today,* women cite their husbands' abuse of alcohol and other substances as the number two reason they got divorced. The number-one reason is physical or emotional abuse, and many times *that* is fueled by alcohol.

So, again, big ups to you in the areas of your life where you are staying strong. We are proud of you, and we're not the only ones. As for those other areas, it's time to, with God's help, take back control. This is your life, your God-given body. Treat it with care. Build those abstinence muscles—you're going to need them for the rest of your life on earth.

 **SLICE OF ADVICE:**

"Say 'No' to ungodliness and worldly passions and . . . live self-controlled, upright, and godly lives" (Titus 2:12).

PLEASE, EASY ON THE CHEESE

You've probably heard people justify getting buck-wild on spring break or a long road trip or summer vacation with platitudes like "What happens in Cancun stays in Cancun" or "What happens on the Senior Trip stays on the Senior Trip." Reality check: If you get genital herpes in Cancun, guess what's going to follow you all the way home to Topeka (or wherever)? If you get pregnant in Vegas, the baby won't miraculously disappear when you cross the state line. You get the point, right? What happens in _____ stays with you, in your heart, your mind, maybe even your bloodstream, for a long time.

 **DELIVER ON THIS:**

Right now, think of an area of your life in which you are doing the right thing. Maybe you've always had control in this area; maybe you recently regained control. Allow yourself at least a few moments to feel good about this, because you should. Now, take the next step. If there is an area in which you struggle, think how cool it would be to think of this area as a Win, not a Loss. What can you do to move that "L" over to the "W" column? Start right now.

RIGHT GUARD FOR GOD?

If you read the Bible, you'll find a lot of physical imagery used to explain God—even though he is a spirit and is beyond flesh and bones. But in order to help us flesh-and-bone folk understand our Creator, the biblical writers talk about God's hands, his eyes, even his wings.

But you won't find a single verse using this image: the sweat glands of God. That's because God doesn't sweat. He doesn't get tired or suffer from aching muscles. He never gets stressed out, despite the size of a task. He doesn't enter his mansion after a hard millennium's work and say, "Whew-boy, I sure could use a hot shower, a couple Advil, and a mentholated rubdown from an angel!"

God is superhuman, tireless, and all-powerful. Yet what did he do after creating the world? He rested. Let that sink into your brain. God rested. He didn't need to rest, but he purposefully took the time to step back, cease working, and enjoy his creation. If an all-powerful being made time to rest, that should speak volumes to us mere mortals.

As a member of the human race, you need to rest occasionally. Yeah, you're young and you have lots to do. You have plenty of adrenaline—and maybe plenty of Red Bull—flowing through your veins and you feel indestructible, indefatigable.

You still need to chill sometimes. You need to focus on "human" once in a while, and not so much on "race." You need to take time to recover physically, emotionally, and spiritually from life's demands. You need time to take stock of where you've been, where you are, and where you are headed. You need quiet, reflective, and restful moments—away from stress and assignments and to-do lists. You need to take the time to be a friend, a son or daughter, a brother or sister, a child of God.

It's ironic that while most of the animal kingdom has figured out this principle, many of the so-called more advanced creatures haven't. Japan's snow monkeys, for example, work hard just to stay alive in their frigid habitat. They must climb high mountains continuously as they search for food. But they take frequent breaks to rest and renew themselves, even monkey around a little. They seem to have an innate understanding that all work and no play leads to exhaustion—and maybe extinction.

Contrast the monkeys to many of Japan's human workers, who have literally worked themselves to death. We are not kidding about this. Some of them are even dropping dead at their desks. The drive for performance—exemplified not only by output, but also by hours put in—permeates the Japanese work culture. This tragic syndrome has become so prevalent that it's been given its own name: karoshi.

It's possible to become so obsessed with work, school, or extracurricular activities that you ignore your body's physical and mental signals that rest and replenishment are needed. It's not wise to disregard those signals. Various studies—including a recent one at the University of Chicago—reveal that those who fail to recharge their mental and physical batteries once in a while are more susceptible to illness and stress-related problems such as ulcers—and to mistakes on the job. Rest can help you avoid such perils.

Additionally, in resting you will find the time and the right frame of mind to contemplate God's wonders and to thank him for his grace and kindness to you. And you can gather the energy to live your life to the fullest.

There's no question—you need rest to be at your best. But rest can be elusive. How can you fit some down time into an already crowded life?

Here are a few tips:

First, build rest time into your daily schedule. Let's face it, if you're like many teens, that's the only way you'll refrain from nonstop homework, sports, or music practice, even church-related activity. And it's okay to be a bit selfish, a bit inflexible about this rest time. If you aren't, something else will crowd it out. Take a regular ten-minute head-clearing walk after lunch or at break time (if you have a job). Or read a book for pleasure, not as an assignment. Or just use those minutes as chill time. One businessperson we know goes to his car every afternoon, reclines his seat, and grabs a fifteen-minute power nap.

Another great way to take a load off is to pursue interests and hobbies that differ from what you do at school or on the job. And in this case, adopting a favorite TV show can count as an "interest." (Please, just don't let it be *Jerry Springer*.) This strategy can help you engage and feed your brain and body in a way that your school or job does not. At the same time, it will give those often-used job- and academic-related parts a needed respite.

Finally, get adequate sleep at night. Your body needs it. Your mind needs it. Sure, you might be able to get more work done if you sleep fewer hours each night, but at what cost? Turn off the TV. Shut down the computer. Close the textbook. Sleep.

To be at your best, to be healthy, to be a well-rounded person, to fully and truly enjoy life, you must find the time to rest your body, mind, and spirit. Think of all the extra hours you spend working and studying—and worrying about school or work. Think of what that time could mean to your family, your friends, your well-being, and your relationship with God—the God who understands the value of occasional rest time. Jesus said, "Come to me, all you who are weary and burdened, and I will give you rest" (Matthew 11:28). Take him up on that offer.

 ## SLICE OF ADVICE:

"Ask where the good way is, and walk in it, and you will find rest for your souls" (Jeremiah 6:16). Wondering where that good way is? It's the road that's not clogged with traffic. It's the path on which you can proceed slowly. It's the way that leads to a place—both literally and figuratively—of peace and quiet and reflection.

 ## DELIVER ON THIS:

Remember that first tip five paragraphs ago? Take us up on it. Find a way to build some downtime into your life every day. You have to make this time happen, and you must protect it—or something will gobble it up. If you'll do this, we promise that you won't feel so whupped all the time, you'll have more energy and enthusiasm, and you'll have a healthier, more positive perspective on life.

THE LOW-DOWN ON FEELING DOWN LOW

Emotions are wonderful. They add flavor, fun, and heat to life. They make us feel alive. Unfortunately, at times they can also make us feel less alive—or like we don't want to live at all. They can even make us believe that no one, including God, loves us.

In our many years of working with teens and preteens, we have seen despair and depression drive people to substance abuse, eating disorders, running away, even suicide.

We write about this topic with a healthy dose of fear. We aren't clinical psychologists or experts in the field of human emotions. You might be saying, "Who are you to tell me how to deal with my depression?" That is a valid question.

The thing is, we have seen too many people sink so low emotionally that they have damaged or ended their lives. We can't duck this topic.

Still, before we tackle this one, we have to do something we dislike: issue a disclaimer. But we promise not to do it in that rapid-fire manner you hear at the end of car and cell-phone commercials.

What we'll present in a few moments are some tools to help you handle despair, depression, the blues—whatever you want to call it. These have worked for us and teens we have counseled. However, we aren't trying to replace your parents, school guidance counselor, youth leader, or pastoral counselor. And we aren't trying to supplant your psychologist or psychiatrist. If you feel that you have an ongoing problem with depression, please talk to someone who is available, qualified, and equipped to help you. There might be chemical factors behind your depression. Or you might have issues from your past that need to be resolved.

That said, here come the suggestions. We hope they can help you and supplement the guidance and support you get from qualified people around you.

TOOLS FOR DEALING WITH DESPAIR

1. Get a new point of view—literally. This may sound too simplistic, but try it sometime. If you are lying in your bed, staring at the ceiling, and failing to see the point in life (and sinking lower and lower by the minute), find a new space. And we don't just mean a new head space. Go outside, for example, even if it's cold. Breathe fresh air. Stargaze. Listen to the sounds of the night. You just might find your perspective changing.

Why does this work? We're just not sure. Maybe it's because a bedroom or any room in a house or apartment can seem like a prison cell when you're depressed. The walls start to press in on you. But once you're outside, you see that the world is way bigger than your room. And, for us, staring up at the night sky reminds us that there is a world beyond the one we experience now, a world full of hope and joy and love.

2. Give yourself some time. This is similar to point number 1. Just as a change in physical location can make a world of difference in one's perspective, so too can the passing of time. If you or a friend is ever thinking about finally having it out with a parent, running away, getting high,

or even ending life, our advice, our plea, is . . . WAIT. Give it time.

We've seen people make terrible mistakes and decisions—and say hateful, destructive things at 1 A.M., in a claustrophobic house, after a long, stress-filled day—made worse by inadequate sleep and food. Again, we're not trying to reduce life's crises to something that can be solved with "a nice hot meal and a good night's sleep," but we're not discounting those things either. Think about it: Have you ever been deeply saddened or bitterly angry late at night, only to find that, when morning came, your whole outlook changed and what seemed an uncrossable ocean was really just the kiddie pool at the Holiday Inn?

3. Remember your history. If you have lived on this earth for even twelve or thirteen years, you've known what it's like to experience sadness or despair or bewilderment that seemed permanent. Maybe you have watched, as we have, a parent or a close friend die and said to yourself, "I don't know how I will ever smile or be able to truly enjoy life again. I honestly don't know how I am supposed to go on after something like this." But somehow you did it, didn't you? In time, you smiled again, laughed again, lived again. You were able to find joy. You were able to comfort others who suffered the way you did. And you were able to get to this precise moment in your life—right now—with enough energy, enough hope, to be reading a book that was prayerfully written to help you and those around you find at least a few keys to living a more fulfilling life. (And we are deeply grateful that you are here sharing this moment with us.)

We're not sure how you got here—maybe *you* should write a book and tell the world—but we ask that you remember and appreciate that you did, because it's likely that someday you'll face a new challenge—or the "Revenge of the Old Challenge." And, once again, you will be tempted to give up hope. But be a history major, okay, if only for a few moments? Remember that you have felt this way before—this depressed, this angry, this confused, or this whatever. But then you felt better. Then you uncovered some answers. Then God brought you peace. Then you met that heaven-sent friend. Then you remembered the people who love you and depend on you. Then you remembered those goals for your life. You remembered, and you got through it. Remember to do that next time, okay?

4. Ask Art's help. No, Art isn't some new self-help guru, the next Dr. Phil. We are talking about the beauty and power of art to inspire the mind and heal the soul. Maybe you can find comfort, as we do, in the soothing, almost other-worldly beauty of the voices of singers like Nichole Nordeman, Eva Cassidy, Out of Eden, or Superchic(k)'s Tricia and Melissa Brock. Or the guitar work of Phil Keaggy or Christopher Parkening.

Maybe it's hip-hop or hard music that rings beautiful to your ears. That's cool too. If beauty is in the eye of the beholder, why can't it be in the ears?

If music isn't your thing, how about the printed word? The warm encouragement of Max Lucado. The joy of one of King David's praise Psalms. The grace-full transparency of Brennan Manning.

Whatever the case, experiencing the lovingly crafted art of a favorite singer, writer, musician, painter, or poet can draw you into God's healing presence. They can be instru
ments of his grace and mercy and peace. They can be like a comforting visit from an old friend. And in hard times, you need a friend.

5. Reach out to a friend. Speaking of friends, they don't just come in the form of music, books, and the like. Think about it: Among your circle of friends, immediate family, extended family, teachers, and other leaders, aren't there at least a few people you could turn to no matter what the problem—or the hour of day or night? Don't worry about being a bother or a nuisance. We'll bet you're a 24/7 kind of friend to some people in your life; let them be the same for you.

6. Help somebody. Find someone in need and pour yourself into making things better for that person. We know that this piece of advice might sound off-point. After all, *you're* the one who needs help. Why—and how—are you supposed to be able to do anyone else any good? We're not sure why this works, but we promise it does. Maybe it's the way it takes the focus off of yourself. Maybe it's how

helping someone else makes you realize that you are important in another's life. Maybe it's healing to see how your own pain helps you empathize more deeply with someone else. It could be all of the above. But, as we said, it works. And it works wonders.

SLICE OF ADVICE:

Remember these words from Isaiah 49:13: "For the Lord comforts his people and will have compassion on his afflicted ones." Remember that the verse says *will* have, not *might* have. It's a promise, not a mere possibility.

DELIVER ON THIS:

The next time you or someone you care about is fighting The Battle of the Blues, try one of the six suggestions in this chapter. Try them all if you have to. Based on our experience, they should help. We aren't saying they will completely solve your problem, but they should help sustain you until you can find the personal, professional help you may need.

THE WORRY SNAKE

We have a confession to make. We try to be good people, but we admit that we can't help watching "those" particular TV channels. You know the ones—they broadcast lots and lots of graphic, gratuitous violence and animalistic sex. That's right: We're hooked on nature channels. Discovery. National Geographic. Animal Planet. You name it.

The other day we saw a particularly brutal show, featuring an anaconda that had captured an unfortunate deer. The deer struggled to escape, but every time it moved, it merely allowed the anaconda's coils to tighten, slowly squeezing the life from another young cousin of Bambi. Soon, the deer was lunch.

Worry can be like that anaconda. Your doubts about your own abilities, your uncertainty about others' feelings toward you, your anxieties about what might happen in the future—they become like reptilian coils that surround you and squeeze the energy and hope out of you. And the more you struggle against them, the tighter those coils constrict.

Want to avoid the crushing, oppressive power of The Worry Snake? Want to keep your anxieties from dominating your life? You have two weapons at your disposal: The first is perspective (yes, *again*); the other is peace. Think of them as two clubs you can use to beat that worrisome snake on the head when it slithers up to you.

The Apostle Paul, who wrote much of the Bible's New Testament, was a man who possessed perspective. He instructed fellow believers to be "anxious for nothing." Think about those words. Paul says we shouldn't worry about *anything*! And he didn't give this advice flippantly. He was in prison when he wrote it. In fact, he spent lots of time in various dirt-bag dungeons, where he was beaten, clamped in chains, and separated from those he loved.

Beyond these trials, Paul had some type of "thorn in the flesh," a physical condition that pained him so much that he asked God repeatedly to cure him. God, in this case, said no.

When he wasn't in jail, Paul was getting shipwrecked, bitten by a poisonous snake, and pelted with stones by people who didn't appreciate his outspoken faith. Ultimately, his belief in God got him beheaded.

So when a guy like this tells us not to worry, we should listen. And we should emulate the kind of perspective he had. Paul knew what was truly important. He knew God loved him and had a plan for his life.

God loves you too. He has a plan for your life. And that plan doesn't include being consumed by worry. So maintain the right perspective. Will the world stop turning if you don't quite make straight A's or don't get named all-conference in sports or music? Will babies no longer giggle and birds no longer sing if you don't get into your number-one college choice or you don't lose the ten pounds you hope to shed this year?

What is a traffic ticket or flat tire or late assignment or cold sore or a zit outbreak compared with being loved purely and eternally by Almighty God and being made clean from all of your sins?

Paul operated his life from this kind of heavenly perspective—a perspective that gave him *peace* (there's your club number two), despite all the painful trials he endured. (By the way, we know we named a club "peace." We kinda like the paradox. We used to have a goldfish named Dusty.)

Paul learned a key truth about peace: God doesn't always untie all the knots—those things that make us worry. But in these cases, the Heavenly Father does give his children the grace to live with the knots.

So remember, there is nothing you face that is too difficult, too troubling, or too frightening for God. God doesn't have sweat glands, remember? Problems don't keep him up at night—he's awake and on the job all of the time.

Use this knowledge of God's power to transform worry time into an opportunity to seek God's perspective, God's peace, the way Paul did.

When he was in jail, for example, instead of worrying about how he was being treated or when he would be released, he wrote letters of encouragement and instruction to people he knew—to large groups of believers and to individual friends. He sang hymns of praise to God. In at least one case, he led his jailer to a saving faith.

You can follow Paul's lead. If, for example, you and some of your friends fear getting cut from a sports team, don't spend your days and nights fretting over what might happen—and when it might happen to you. Do your best work during tryouts. Determine a contingency plan in the event you don't make the roster. Help your friends develop action plans of their own. Be someone with whom they can share their fears and anxieties. Encourage one another. It's amazing how helping others can eliminate worry and stress.

And don't forget to tell God how you feel. Thank him for all that he's given you and seek his wisdom for your future.

God loves you. He cares about your life. And he is completely capable of carrying your worries. So the next time you feel worry squeezing the life out of you, remember the words of Paul, the physically impaired, oft-jailed martyr: "The Lord is near. Do not be anxious about anything, but in everything, by prayer and petition, with thanksgiving, present your requests to God. And the peace of God, which transcends all understanding, will guard your hearts and your minds in Christ Jesus" (Philippians 4:5–7).

Never forget that a peace that can transcend all understanding can certainly transcend worry too.

 **SLICE OF ADVICE:**

"Therefore do not worry about tomorrow, for tomorrow will worry about itself. Each day has enough trouble of its own" (Matthew 6:34).

 **DELIVER ON THIS:**

When you hear the word "habit," you might immediately associate it with "bad." But habits can just as easily be good. We want you to adopt one of those for this delivery. You will encounter worry in life; there's no way to control that. You can, however, control your response to worry. The next time you feel worry wrapping its coils around you, don't start pacing the floor and focusing on what an awful bind you're in. Don't start playing out worst-case scenarios in your mind, like movie previews. Instead, turn first to God. Every time. All the time. Rest in his love. Seek his guidance, whether through prayer, reading the Bible or a book, or consulting a pastor or youth leader. Maybe you'll want to do all of the above.

If you will do this, you will find that those coils just won't be able to grip and squeeze you. The Worry Snake will be forced to slither away, worrying about how he's "losing it."

THE GOLDEN RULE: STILL GOOD AS GOLD

Allow us to go old school again for just a little bit. (Come on, we're no longer young and cool. Humor us.)

We want to talk about the Golden Rule—you know—"Do unto others as you would have them do unto you." How long has it been since you've heard someone talk about this? A long time? We were afraid of that.

It seems to us that the Golden Rule isn't what it used to be. Bumper stickers proclaim permutations like "Do Unto Others *Before* They Do Unto You!" or "Do Unto Others—Then Split." Motivational speakers talk about Winning Through Intimidation, and business leaders and professional sports coaches read books like *The Art of War* for inspiration and guidance.

To some people, the Golden Rule has outlived its usefulness. Or it applies only toward being kind, loving, and compassionate to the people who show those characteristics to us—or to those who can help us achieve our personal or professional goals.

The Bible begs to differ. It teaches us to treat *everyone* the way we wish to be treated. Think about that the next time you encounter the various fund-raising groups in front of your local grocery store. Imagine that it was you trying to raise money for something. How would you feel about getting repeated "No-thank-yous" or hostile glares—or being ignored altogether?

What if you began to view every Salvation Army Santa, every church bake-sale table, every confused underclassman in the school hallways, as not an annoyance but an opportunity to show the same kindness, generosity, and compassion that you would like to receive?

But the Golden Rule doesn't stop with those who might merely inconvenience us; it includes our enemies. And is there any tougher commandment than "Love your enemies"? Not tolerate them or simply do kind things for them. Love them. Those obnoxious, cruel, hateful people. The teacher or coach who treats you unfairly. The person who pretends to be your friend, then backstabs you. The relative who is consistently rude and insulting.

The first step in loving our enemies is praying for them (not for their disgracement, downfall, or destruction, by the way). And when we pray for our enemies, we need to pray as much for our own attitudes and behaviors as for theirs. That way, even if our prayers don't change our enemies' ugly qualities, they will change us.

Often the first thing to pray for, by the way, is simply the will and grace to *want* to love those we find unlovable.

In praying for these people, we may come to realize that they are no less attractive to God, no less deserving of his love, than we are. Further, as we experience what hard work it is to love unlovable people, we will value God's love for us more than ever.

And finally, as we practice "Do Unto Others," we might actually turn an enemy into a friend—or at least someone who is neutral rather than hostile.

Whatever the case, whether the change happens in others or only in ourselves, when we obey the Golden Rule, we invariably find that it's still as good as gold.

 ## SLICE OF ADVICE:

"So in everything, do to others what you would have them do to you, for this sums up the Law and the Prophets" (Matthew 7:12). A quick note here: This is a direct quote from Jesus. This is advice to be heeded. Remember, it's called The Golden Rule, not The Golden Suggestion.

 ## DELIVER ON THIS:

Right now, think of a person you have trouble dealing with, maybe even your arch-nemesis, the Green Goblin to your Spider-Man. Resolve that during your next encounter with this person, you will put the Golden Rule into action. It will be hard to do; we're not going to kid you about this. But if you *commit* to obeying the Rule right now, you'll have a much better chance of actually obeying it later.

THE FRIENDSHIP FACTOR

You probably possess one of life's rarest treasures right now, and you may not know it. No, it's not your winning smile or your CD collection (although we bet both are impressive).

If you have a friend, especially someone you call a best friend, you are blessed. Absolutely blessed. Please don't ever take friendship for granted.

We left high school behind a long time ago, and we've discovered something in the years since: The friends you make as teens—or even younger—might be the best friends you'll ever have. Yes, you will probably meet some fascinating people in your future. You will work with them, play sports with them, maybe even play Bunco or golf with them, if that becomes your thing someday.

But there is something about friendships that are forged in our younger years. Maybe there's a special bond between people who endure puberty—and algebra classes—together. We're not sure if that's the secret. We wish we were smart enough to explain the mystery of it, but you'll just have to trust us. Who knows? Maybe it's because adult corporate America, with its frantic pace, posturing, and competition, doesn't exactly foster true friendship.

Even in the best corporate environments, you see a lot of "colleagues" and "associates" and "counterparts," but few true friends.

Take a few moments to think about a best friend or two. Sure, they have faults. And you might think them predictable and uninteresting. Maybe they have hurt you, or vice versa. But think about the months, even the years, you have invested in these friendships. Think about what you love about your best buds. The adventures you've shared. The times you stood up for each other. The great stories. The laughs. The understanding. The compliments. The favors they have done for you.

Take it from two guys who have lost close friends to accidents. Treasure your friends. Don't pass up an opportunity to tell them, or show them, that you appreciate how much they mean to your life. Be there for them when they need you, the way you hope they'll be there for you. Perhaps you already know—you don't have to hope or imagine.

Pray for their safety and well-being too. Couldn't hurt, might help.

You will do cool things in your life. If you seek God's guidance, you will find a calling custom-tailored just for you. That calling may include a rewarding job, a loving family. But right now, you are called to be a friend. You'll hear the same call in the future. And whatever you end up doing in your life, it's doubtful there will be a nobler calling than being a true friend to someone.

 **DOUBLE SLICE OF ADVICE:**

1. "A friend loves at all times" (Proverbs 17:17).
2. "Do not forsake your friend" (Proverbs 27:10).

DELIVER ON THIS:

Think of your best friend. And now—right now—do something good for him or her. It might just be a simple phone call or e-mail. Maybe a surprise visit—with your bud's favorite dessert in hand—is in order. Perhaps you want to do something bigger, such as ordering a book or CD. Most likely, you know just what you should do. Do it now. Don't feel weird about it. Remember how we mentioned those friends of ours who died? We didn't sit there at any of the funerals thinking, "You know, I really did *too many* nice things for this person." We didn't have any regrets about any compliment, favor, or gift. You won't either. Even if you and your friends live to be one hundred.

Seriously, go now. Stop reading this and go!

CAN YOU GO THE DISTANCE?

Watch a televised marathon and you'll see an interesting phenomenon. As the starter's gun fires, a few novice runners will sprint to the front of the pack. These attention-grabbers want a few moments on camera—and they want to be able to boast to friends, "I led the marathon! I was in first place!"

However, while these people might get the attention they crave at the start of the race, you probably won't see them crossing the finish line 26.2 miles later—unless they are walking. That's because they know how to get a fast start, but they can't finish strong. Finishing a marathon requires patience, perspective, endurance, strength, and just plain grit. It's a lot like life itself.

Almost anyone can approach life's endeavors with an initially high level of energy and enthusiasm. Unfortunately, many of these endeavors can drain one's energy and flatten one's enthusiasm. The truly successful people are those who can maintain their commitment to a goal over the long haul.

You can bring a champion marathoner's approach to your life's goals—ensuring that you will start fresh and finish strong—by following the three Ps.

The first key is preparation. Remember those glory-hound runners from the first paragraph? They couldn't finish the race they started so briskly because they weren't prepared for the long challenge before them. They didn't train well or adapt a special diet to prepare their bodies. They didn't read books or articles on marathoning or formulate a race plan to ensure they were mentally ready.

Preparation can help you succeed at any endeavor. If, for example, you want to lose a few pounds (for the right reasons, okay?), prepare yourself by reading what qualified people have to say about the subject. Talk with family members or friends who have been successful about shedding weight and keeping it off. Seek their advice. Enlist their support.

The second key is perspective. (Hey, have you gotten the idea that this concept is really important?) A marathoner realizes that he has a long race before him, so he doesn't get caught up in the early excitement and expend too much energy at the beginning. He paces himself. Todd is the marathoner of the Hafer brothers (Jedd is the smart one), and he strives for a "negative split" when he runs a marathon. This means he sets out to run the second half of the race faster than the first.

That's because of a longtime racing axiom that warns: For every minute you run too fast in the first half of the race, you will lose twice that amount in the second half. You can adapt the same principle of balance and perspective. In school, for example, don't load up on too many hard classes in one quarter or semester. Try to build a schedule that's balanced. You can apply the same principle on a smaller level. When you're preparing for a test, don't leave all the mental "heavy lifting" for the night before.

Perspective doesn't just help you handle the work at hand; it also helps you develop a proper attitude toward that work. When a marathoner hits the midpoint of his race, for example, he doesn't think, *Oh no, I still have a long way to go!* Instead, he tells himself, *All right! I've already come a long way. From this point, I don't even have to run a marathon anymore—it's just a half marathon!*

The final "P" is perseverance. Almost any goal requires perseverance. That's because almost any goal will present obstacles and disappointments. Even with all the preparation and perspective in the world, you may reach a point of mental and physical fatigue as you strive to finish what you've started.

Times like these require good old-fashioned staying power. Willpower. Determination. You'll face moments when you must remind yourself of what your goal is, how much it means to you, and how you will feel if you don't achieve it. Then you take one more stride, eat one more carrot stick (instead of a Twinkie), read one more chapter, take one more test. Perseverance isn't always pretty, but it works. Just ask Thomas Edison, who failed a thousand times before coming up with a properly functioning light bulb.

You might not have the lung capacity of an elite marathon runner or the scientific acumen of an Edison, but you can match their determination. And when you finish what you've begun, you can share in their triumph as well.

 ## DOUBLE SLICE OF ADVICE:

1. "Let us run with perseverance the race marked out for us. Let us fix our eyes on Jesus, the author and perfecter of our faith" (Hebrews 12:1–2).
2. "Blessed is the man who perseveres under trial" (James 1:12).

 **DELIVER ON THIS:**

The next time you find yourself getting discouraged about your progress toward a long-term goal, try to focus on the whole goal, not just the current piece of it that is dragging you down. Tell yourself that over the long haul, you will have the opportunity to correct mistakes and make up for lost time. Remind yourself of how far you have already progressed and be encouraged by this fact: The distance between you and your goal is less than it was when you started—maybe a lot less.

YOU CAN PREVENT TRUTH DECAY

There are so many roads up the mountain, but the view from the top is still the same."

"There are no absolutes."

"It doesn't matter what you believe, as long as you sincerely believe something."

Have you heard clichés like these? If not, you will. The "T" word—tolerance—is in vogue right now. That's not necessarily a bad thing. We should respect differing viewpoints, different customs. However, it is entirely possible—in fact it's entirely necessary—to respectfully *disagree* when you are confronted with a lie masquerading as the truth, a mere theory masquerading as proven fact.

Thus, here's our plea to you: As you search and sift through the various messages that the media, friends, and teachers hurl at you, let us make one small suggestion: Find the truth. Don't make life decisions based on lies, opinions, wishes, or theories. Theories and the like are fine to consider, to discuss. But they make a lousy foundation on which to base your life.

For example, some people respond to the question, "Where will you go when you die?" with something like, "Whatever you believe about life after death will come true for you. If you believe in heaven, you'll go to heaven. If you believe in reincarnation, it will happen to you." Really? Is that the way everything else works? If you believe you'll be a world-renowned rock star, is that a guarantee it will happen? Even on a smaller scale, if you sincerely believe in your erroneous answer on a chemistry test, does that make it true?

How foolish to decide how to live our lives on anything less than what is tested and true. Unfortunately, what began as a great idea in our culture—tolerance—has become a reason to validate many ideas, even those that directly contradict one another. This is a logical impossibility. While it is admirable to give differing ideas a fair chance, that doesn't mean all of them are equally true or correct. To paraphrase our buddy Steve Taylor, it's unwise to be so open-minded that your brains tumble out.

Truth is singular. It's exclusive. Many in popular culture wimp out: "What's true for you might not be true for me," they say. Really? If we say the capital of Wyoming is Laramie, does that make us right? No way. (Just in case you're not up on the cowboy state, the correct answer is Cheyenne.)

Let's raise the stakes now—far beyond the answer to a geography test. If we put our faith in—and follow—some dead human mystic, will the result be the same as if we believe in Jesus Christ, the perfect Son of the living God? That's like saying, "You pull yourself in a wagon while I board a space shuttle, and we'll both get to the moon just fine." Sorry, wagon-riders, but you have no shot of even getting out of town, no matter how much "faith" or sincerity you have. Faith must be placed in something real and powerful. Something that works. Something that will get us where we need to go. Our faith must be in the truth. And only Jesus is the pure truth.

He said it himself, "I am the way, the truth, and the life. No one comes to the Father except through me." He didn't say "a way," or even "one of the best ways." And if you have a Bible concordance, check it out sometime and see how many times Jesus prefaced a statement with "I tell you the truth." Clearly, the concept was, and is, important to him.

Not so in twenty-first-century America. And that's why biblical Christianity is everyone's whipping boy these days. It's one of the few things you can knock on national TV and get everyone to nod and applaud. You've heard the criticisms: "Christians are insecure, narrow-minded, intolerant fanatics who think they are better than everyone else." "What makes Christianity any better than all the other religions?" "Christians need to lighten up and give other religions their due."

Unfortunately, Christianity just isn't a "lighten up" kind of thing. It's rooted in a supreme bloody sacrifice by the incarnate Son of God. Christians have been murdered for their beliefs for the past two thousand years, and it's still happening today. Why? For seeking the truth—for proclaiming and living out the truth.

The Bible promises that God rewards those who seek him. That's what we encourage you to do. Seek God, because God is truth; God is love. You shouldn't be arrogant in your quest for the truth or your supposed understanding of it. We are all seekers, and we doubt that any one denomination or school of religious thought has perfectly understood God's truth.

Let's all trust in God's promise that he will reward us if we seek him. We don't all have to quit our current churches and join the one that claims to be the closest to the truth—or to have the "Truth Market" cornered. We know Catholic people who are earnestly, honestly seeking God. We know people who are hungry for God but don't attend *any* church at the moment. We know sincere Christian Democrats, sincere Christian Republicans. It would be arrogant of us to say that any of these honest seekers have no chance of finding the One they seek. What unites these people is that they are hungry for the truth. That's why we believe they will realize the promise of "seek and ye shall find."

It would be different if they were using their church—or lack thereof—as an excuse to run away from the truth or ignore it. But that's not the case.

You might think that a quest for the truth is too tiring, too burdensome. But that's not the case, really. It takes effort and study and prayer to "rightly divide the word of truth," but it is worth the effort. Because, as Jesus said, "The truth will set you free." Ever wonder "free from what?" How about free from lies, free from contradictory theories, free from double-talk, free from prideful thinking, free from the fickle winds of popular opinion, free from hype?

In a world of lies and smoke and mirrors, it's pure freedom to have something to depend on, something to put your back up against. And that's the Truth.

 ## SLICE OF ADVICE:

"Do your best to present yourself to God as one approved, a workman who does not need to be ashamed and correctly handles the word of truth" (2 Timothy 2:15).

 ## DELIVER ON THIS:

Start to view your Bible as your Truth Measuring Stick. You will hear a lot of theories and philosophies that sound good, seem reasonable. But things aren't always as they seem. So before you change your viewpoint about something—or take a course of action—go back to the Book. Talk to someone whom you admire for his or her knowledge of and respect for the Bible and biblical history. You might find that what looks fresh and attractive on the surface is rotten underneath.

YOU DON'T HAVE TO BE THE TOP DOG, DAWG

Reality TV" is one of our favorite oxymorons. In fact, this term may be the most oxymoronic oxymoron in the history of oxymoronism! That's because Reality TV has about as much to do with reality as Cheez-Its have to do with an actual dairy product.

But this chapter isn't a true rant about Reality TV—although the subject is begging for one. It's about the way Reality TV contributes to a winner-take-all viewpoint of life. Think about how the shows are named. *Last Comic Standing. Elimidate. Survivor* (not *Survivors*). *American Idol* (not *Idols*). Even though *The Weakest Link* positions itself a bit differently, the result is the same. At some point during this show, all but one participant will be *The Weakest Link,* leaving the show with no money. How's that for parity? Almost everyone has to be "Weakest." Only one is ultimately deemed to be "Strong."

Think about how these shows are set up: Thousands try out. A handful actually get on the air. But how many get to win? One. What about all of those other people who go home "losers"? Are they really losers? Are they failures?

The all-or-nothing mentality sets up most people for failure. It's a cruel system. What makes it even more cruel is how the shows troll for contestants—challenging them to test their intellects, talents, athleticism, attractiveness, and resourcefulness, promising fame, big bucks, or a mate (for contestants or even their *dad*)!

"Are you The Next Big Whatever?" the shows' marketers ask breathlessly. "If you believe in yourself and have what it takes, you just might be!"

We say "enough" to these shallow appeals to people's egos and desire for fame and money. When did becoming The Next Big Thing become the ultimate goal? More important, *why*?

Here's the real juice: God didn't call you to be the Rock Star All-Being / No. 1 Media Icon / Hottie Master of All You Survey. He called you to be one thing: faithful. And if you are faithful to him, you get to be precisely what he wants you to be, not necessarily what *you* want to be. Right now, there are approximately half a gazillion teens who really, really, want to be the next American Idol, the next NBA all-star, or the next box-office sensation. But those kinds of honors aren't handed out indiscriminately like Halloween candy (or Fall Harvest candy, if you're a conservative Baptist).

We know right now that some of you are saying, "Oh, ye Hafer brothers of little faith. I will be The Next Big Thing. Just you watch!"

The problem is, while you are thinking this, so are thousands of other "exceptions to the rule." And there can't be thousands of exceptions—that's why they're called exceptions. They're rare. They happen about as infrequently as Halley's Comet appears—or one of our books hits the bestseller lists.

So while everyone else is telling you, "Get Paid," "Get Famous," and "Get Rich," we want to tell you, "Get Real."

You are probably not going to be famous. We've written about thirty books, and we're not famous. Does that bother us? Do we pine to be on the cover of *Newsweek* like Jerry Jenkins? No. Really, no. See, we don't see our job as writing bestselling books or books that grab media headlines. Our job is simply to write the best books we can about topics that matter to us. That's why we're writing this book for you. You matter. We want, more than anything else, to connect with our readers.

We hope that for our publisher's sake, our books make some money. And given that we both have kids who digest food like little blast furnaces, we are grateful for extra help in putting meals on the table.

But really, once we have written the best book we can and strived to serve our readers, the outcome is in bigger hands than ours. When we speak at writers' conferences, we tell attendees, "There are two terrible things that can happen to a writer. The first is writing to chase fame and never catching it. The second is writing to chase fame and actually getting it." This is writing not to serve but rather to be served (or afford servants). The French author Molière said that this approach to writing "is like prostitution. First you do it for love, then you do it for a few friends, and finally you do it for money." What an apt analogy.

We're not saying that you should have no ambition—or that you shouldn't aspire to greatness—it's just a matter of whose idea of greatness. Think about it: Does God want to give you a famous face? Make you a pop idol? Even pimp your ride? Or does he want to save your soul and guide your life?

Here's our sincere hope for you: You *will* do great things. Maybe not great in scope or national notability. But great nonetheless. The kind of greatness that happens whenever the Creator and one of his creations work in concert. You will have a great impact on the lives around you. Maybe even one life. But wouldn't you rather deeply impact one or a few lives than have a passing, transient influence on thousands? Besides, those few lives you impact will reach out to others. You will have left a legacy. And you don't have to be famous, funny, or flush with a fortune to establish a legacy. Just faithful.

 SLICE OF ADVICE:

"Whoever wants to become great among you must be your servant" (Matthew 20:26).

DELIVER ON THIS:

Mother Teresa said, "Every day we are called to do small things with great love." Think of one "small thing with great love" that you can do for someone, or a group of someones, during the next twenty-four hours, then do it. It can be a simple favor, a small random act of kindness. It could be as low-key as putting your spare change in the donation box at your favorite restaurant or snack shop. But even if your gesture is this small, make sure the love you do it with is big.

TIME TO REHEAT IT

It's that time again. Here's the latest, greatest, and micro-wave-safest recap:

1. Work those ab (as in abstinence) muscles. The sex abs. The alcohol abs. The money-spending abs. All of them. Wail on 'em. You will need them for the rest of your natural-born life.

2. Worry and depression can drain joy and hope from your life. Pray that God will give you the proper perspective for dealing with these challenges. And don't hesitate to reach out to a parent, pastor, friend, or counseling professional for help.

3. The Golden Rule ("Do unto others . . .") is still the Gold Standard for human interaction.

4. Friendship rocks. A Nigerian proverb we really like says, "Hold on to a true friend with both of your hands." That's good advice.

5. Have yourself "committed." To achieve anything significant in life, you need to be committed to achieving your goal. There is no substitute for pure, old-fashioned perseverance, the ability to keep your shoulder to the wheel even when your strength fades.

6. Seek the truth. Be humble in your quest, but not timid. Don't believe the notion that one person's opinion is just as good as another's. It's a generous notion, to be sure, but there's one problem: God doesn't have opinions, just truth.

7. Don't let your ambition run amok. Keep that beast on a leash. Don't believe the hype that you have to be The Next Big Whatever to make your mark in life. All you have to be is faithful. Be wary of anything or anyone that panders to your ego, your pride. Because C. S. Lewis said it well, pride is "the complete anti-God state of mind."

8. Rest once in a while. If it was good enough for God, it's good enough for you. So rest, recharge, renew.

LET'S TALK ABOUT SEX

You might hear various leaders telling you not to think about sex so much. We sure have. "Too many teens have sex on the brain," they say. "Teens need to spend less time thinking and talking about sex and more time occupying themselves with other things. Like memorizing Habakkuk."

We respectfully disagree with these people. At the risk of receiving hate mail from lots of adults, we think teens probably need to think about sex *more*. Talk about it more. That's right. We don't mean obsess on it in an unhealthy way. We don't mean swap off-color jokes—or nudie jpegs—with your friends. But we do mean more serious, thoughtful consideration and conversation.

Why? Because we believe the number one reason that so many "good kids" get into trouble sexually is that the topic isn't talked about. It's hurriedly shoved into the broom closet and commanded, "Don't you dare show yourself until these hapless teens are thirty-five, at least!" This is stupid. Look at what happens in the real world: Many MTV videos look like underwear ads. Underwear ads, in turn, look like soft-core porn . . . and you get the picture. Sometimes literally. Speaking of porn, know how many pornographic Web sites lurk on the Internet? According to *Newsweek* magazine, four million.

But you don't have to go looking for sex on the Net. It will find you, even via televised football. We have to admit, we never thought we'd see the day when, while watching Super Bowl commercials with our families, we'd have to turn to our barely-in-grade-school kids and answer the question, "Daddy, what's an erection that lasts more than four hours?" (Hey, *thanks*, Cialis, for helping us make a memorable family moment.)

The point is, *everybody* is talking about sex, it seems—except the followers of the God who invented the concept. That's right, the people who should best be able to understand and appreciate the mystery, the God-given gift of sex, are afraid to talk about it. Not only is this ironic and puzzling, it's dangerous. Christian adults' habit of avoiding honest conversation about sex is one reason so many Christian teens get blindsided by temptation and fall prey to it.

Christian teens need to think about situations they might find themselves in, about pressures they might face. They need to understand that virginity can be a badge of honor and courage, not something akin to a giant L (for loser) branded on their foreheads. They need to know that oral sex is, in fact, sex. (It even has the word "sex" in its name, for pete's sake—or is it Bill's sake!) Sexual purity should be something you protect with all your resources and willpower, not hang on to via a technicality.

So again, you need to think about sex more. But we'd like to offer a few suggestions for directing your thoughts, a few hows and whys.

1. You need to think about sex because your attitudes and actions (or we hope, lack of action) today will affect the future of your sexuality. For example, right now you need to be thinking of that person you will marry someday—and have great sex with. Yes, we just said "great sex." That's not a typo. God wants you to have great sex. He doesn't want you to have second-rate sex—which is the best that people who don't follow his plan

for sexuality can have. God invented sex. He invented it to be satisfying on a physical, emotional, and spiritual level.

You might have already met your future spouse, your lifetime love. You might be dating this person. The best gift you can give him or her—the best gift you can give yourself—is to enter your lifetime commitment to one another without a bunch of sexual baggage. And sexual baggage usually isn't limited to a couple of small carry-on items. It's big and heavy and bulky. It is very hard to put away and keep out of sight.

We talked with a couple we know who have a marriage-counseling service about this topic. And guess what? The number one reason for strife in the couples they counsel is the guilt, shame, suspicion, fear, jealousy, insecurity, etc., caused by one or both partner's sexual activity before marriage.

For those of you who have already messed up in this area, we don't want you to give up hope, because God's grace and forgiveness can work miracles. But that doesn't negate the joy people will experience—and the heartbreak they will avoid— by giving their marriage a clean start.

2. Speaking of clean, there is something else to be gained by staying pure. Let's talk about STDs for just a moment. Remember what we said earlier in the book? Four million teens get infected with an STD every year. That's equivalent to the entire populations of Montana, South Dakota, Wyoming, Alaska, Vermont, and North Dakota combined. And, get your safety goggles on because we are about ready to smash one of the biggest misconceptions in American society today: It's not only prostitutes and party boys who get syphilis, genital warts, gonorrhea, and AIDS. Nice kids get them. Church kids get them. Church kids get them at church camp.

This information needs to be part of your discussions about sex, and it definitely needs to enter into the equation when you think about sex and contemplate questions like, "How far is too far?" (We'll address that question, by the way, at the end of this devo.)

We had so much fun smashing the STD myth that we want to bust another one. (Goggles still on? Good.) It's not only skanky girls who get pregnant—courtesy of playa guys. Church girls get pregnant. "Nice Christian boys" impregnate them. Sometimes this happens at church camp, or in the bus, RV, or van on the way to or from church camp.

You need to think and talk about this too. Being a Christian won't protect you from the consequences of disobeying God's rules for satisfying sex. Getting pregnant, like getting an STD, is a matter of biology. And biology doesn't care about your church-attendance record or the fact that you do devotions every night.

Before we leave this topic, we need to confront a rebuttal that we hear when we debate this topic on the radio or in classrooms: "You are just trying to scare teens needlessly. A condom will prevent all of that scary stuff you're talking about."

First of all, we don't mind copping to part of this accusation. We *are* trying to plant a healthy dose of fear in you about the consequences of sex. Do we feel guilty about that? Let's ponder that for a moment—nope.

Second, some people talk about condoms the way they talk about Superman. Please. There's only so much a paper-thin layer of latex can do. Now, we're not anti-condom. And at the risk of bringing more parental wrath upon us, we'll tell you straight up that when we counsel teens who are sexually active and have no intention of becoming "inactive," we tell them that they should use protection. But we do this with a heavy heart. Why? Well, take a look at the many things a condom *won't* protect you from:

- A damaged reputation
- Breaking the hearts of people who love you (that includes God)
- Shame and guilt
- The grief of being used
- The loss of innocence
- Disappointment, with yourself and your partner
- STDs
- Pregnancy (This is no misprint. Condoms break. Condoms leak. Condoms get used improperly.)

3. Having mature conversations about sex and devoting time to thinking and praying about it will help you avoid compartmentalizing it as some dark, hidden corner of your life that is never illuminated by godly wisdom or sound advice from other people. Christians are so susceptible to being tripped up by one "dirty little habit" or another. It might be sex or pornography, but it could just as easily be drugs or gambling.

So there you have it: our official permission to think and talk about sex. Please use this permission wisely.

 **SLICE OF ADVICE:**

"Whatever is true, whatever is noble, whatever is right, whatever is pure, whatever is lovely, whatever is admirable—if anything is excellent or praiseworthy—think about such things" (Philippians 4:8). Sexuality, when it's lived out according to the will of the One who invented it, is all of the above, and more. Think about that.

 **DELIVER ON THIS:**

Here is a guide for the age-old "How Far Is Too Far?" question about sex. Please think about the following words the next time you find yourself in a potentially compromising sexual situation—or, better yet, *beforehand*. First of all, "How far?" is the wrong question. You shouldn't ask, "How far can I go without angering God or becoming so carried away that I end up having intercourse?" You should ask, "What is right for me to do at this point in my life, at this point in my relationship? What will honor God and show respect for my partner and myself?"

Here's a second, more specific exercise. As you contemplate what romantic actions are appropriate, imagine that your future spouse is somewhere in the world—in the exact same situation you are in, at the exact same moment. Now, think about what you want him or her to do. Are you okay with some guy kissing your future spouse the way you want to kiss the girl you are with? If not, that's a good indication of what you should—or should not—do. Are you okay with some girl touching your future husband the way you are thinking about touching the guy you're with right now? Kind of clears up the whole "how far" question, doesn't it?

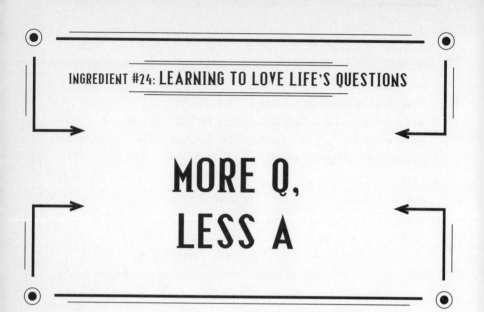

MORE Q, LESS A

Here's a career option for you: Find a subject, become an expert in that subject, then convince people your subject is important to them. For example, maybe you could choose Kung Fu. Kung Fu is important, after all, because people need to be able to defend themselves in this increasingly dangerous world. Besides, Kung Fu can help people get in shape. And let's not forget the uniforms. They look cool, and we bet they are comfortable too.

Once you are a Kung Fu expert, the Kung Fu Answer Person, you'll have hordes of folks Kung Fu Kicking down your door for a slice of your wisdom. That's because people crave answers. We have to know the how, the why, and most important, the "what's in it for me?"

That's why our society has elevated people with answers, from the Shell Answer Man to the Bible Answer Man. (Both are really smart guys, by the way.)

There's a place for good, solid answers, of course. When we ask someone, "Hey, what time is it?" we don't want his eyes to glaze over like Krispy Kreme donuts and hear him say, in a pseudo-philosophical voice, "Whoa, like, who can really say what time it is, dude, and like, what *is* time, really, anyway?"

We don't want to hear mess like that. We just want to know, like, how long until the next SportsCenter, dude?

But on other topics, we are learning to live with, even learn from, life's uncertainties, life's mysteries.

Why did our mom die at a relatively young age when she had always been so health conscious? Why did some of our best friends die suddenly, leaving grieving families, including young children, behind?

We don't know the answers to these questions. And we're learning that it's okay. We're learning that our time and energy and emotions are better spent being thankful for the times we were blessed to share with these people. Better spent honoring their memories—keeping them alive. Better spent comforting others who have been hurt by the loss. Better spent appreciating the people who are still physically with us.

We believe that America's answer obsession is a symptom of something bigger—the attempt to reduce God and all of life to something small and simple enough for our finite minds to understand. But God's ways are not our ways. They are higher and bigger than we can grasp right now.

We get so caught up in reaching a destination called "Complete Understanding" that we forget to enjoy the journey. We forget to enjoy the process and the people who are beside us on our trip.

Think of how many times Jesus spoke in parables or answered one question with another question. Or how he flatly refused when people demanded, "Show us a sign!" Maybe he was trying to teach us something there. Could it be that the quest for understanding, the conversations with God and friends, the exploration, all matter more than arriving at the mistaken notion that we've finally "got it"? Could it be that God's essence cannot be captured in a tiny bottle that we can carry in our pocket?

Maybe it's the search, the journey—not the arrival—that makes us who we are.

We know that life is confusing. But we urge you: Learn to love the questions. Don't worry about getting the definitive answer to all of them. Because as long as you are questioning, you are thinking. Your mind is working. You are praying for understanding. You are being watchful for answers, for truth. We hope you are seeking out others for their insights. All of these things will help you grow as a person, even if you don't get to the final answer.

Life can be mysterious. Learn to love a good mystery.

 SLICE OF ADVICE:

God created us in his image. He doesn't need us to return the favor by shrinking him down to our size or reducing his holy mysteries to bumper-sticker slogans.

 DELIVER ON THIS:

Okay, it's been a while since we asked you to memorize or write down a verse. It's time again. On the surface, this quote from God himself doesn't seem like it would be comforting in a difficult time, but trust us on this one. You won't get so frustrated by your inability to understand something if you can learn to accept that maybe you aren't *supposed* to understand it, at least not right now. Here's the verse: "As the heavens are higher than the earth, so are my ways higher than your ways, and my thoughts than your thoughts" (Isaiah 55:9).

TIME TO SET YOUR PET GRUDGE FREE

Maybe that "pet grudge" was cute when you first got it. But it won't be for long. If you keep feeding it, encouraging it, it will grow big, demanding, and ugly. It will whine and whimper and scratch at your door and keep you up at night. And it will leave unsightly stains on your soul. Bigger and bigger stains. That's because little grudges can grow up to be huge vendettas. So it's time to set that grudge free. The Bible says that a servant of the Lord "must not quarrel; instead, he must be kind to everyone . . . not resentful" (2 Timothy 2:24).

Open your heart's door and shoo the grudge away. Then forgive the person who gave it to you in the first place. You will feel better; we promise. Your heart will feel lighter. And if that grudge ever finds its way back to you and scratches at your door, pretend you are not home.

Remember, if you hold grudges, you won't be able to hold much else.

There's another problem with holding on to a grudge, harboring bitterness and unforgiveness in your heart. And a certain Hafer brother (we'll call him "Todd") provides the perfect illustration. When he was a grade-schooler, Todd thought skunks were cool. He liked their striking black-and-white coloring. He found it amusing that all of God's creatures were afraid of these little animals, just because of the way they smelled. He thought being stinky was a hilarious defense mechanism.

He became so enthralled with skunks that he decided to get a couple as pets—by catching them in the wild. In his tiny second-grade brain, he reasoned that if he found young skunks ("skunk puppies," he called them) and spoke to them in soothing tones and treated them gently, they wouldn't spray him. And, he reasoned, even if they did, young skunks wouldn't be able to produce the kind of eye-stinging stench as the full-grown versions.

He was wrong on all counts. Todd's two new pets, which he dubbed Tinker and Pee-Wee, were cuddly and non-aggressive when he first scooped them into his arms and carried them to their new home, the family milk box. However, the first time he opened the milk-box lid to check on his new pets, he received a double-shot of skunk spray right in the face.

He was not allowed in the house for several hours—hours which included being sprayed down with the garden hose at regular intervals. And even then, it took many rounds in the bathtub, with alternating regimens of tomato juice and Mr. Bubble, before anyone in the family, including our dog, King, would go near him. (And King, it should be noted, regularly rolled in garbage, drank out of the toilet, and dragged home a variety of body parts from dead animals.)

But, and here's the point of this true-life adventure, the skunk stench didn't just pollute Todd and the noses of his family; it affected his own perception of his family—and everything else. His dad didn't smell like Hai Karate and Brylcreem anymore, because Todd's nose could smell only skunk. And his mom's famous cherry pie, which she baked to comfort her son in his hour of need, might as well have been skunk pie, because that's all he could smell or taste.

Bitterness is like concentrated *Eau de Skunk*. It pollutes how we perceive the rest of the world. Pizza doesn't smell and taste as savory when your head is filled with bitterness. The world looks dingy and dark when viewed through lenses smudged and smeared with unforgiveness.

You might have really been hurt. Betrayed. Backstabbed. Lied about. Harassed. Bullied. It stinks, we're not going to lie to you. But you have to let the bitterness go. You need to forgive.

What if the person who hurt you didn't *ask* for forgiveness? What if the person doesn't seem sorry? We hear questions like these whenever we speak about forgiveness. And they are excellent queries.

The best way we can answer them is to point to Jesus' example. Remember what he said when he was bleeding and fighting for breath while dying on the cross? "Father, forgive them, for they know not what they do." Were his tormentors sorry? No. In fact, many of them were mocking him in his time of agony. He forgave them anyway.

How about a different example? Remember the paraplegic man, lowered through a roof by friends—right in front of Jesus? What is the first thing Jesus said to him? "Your sins are forgiven." That wasn't why the guys brought their friend to Jesus. And we believe that the poor man was much more concerned with being able to do the Running Man—even the Walking Man—than having his sins forgiven. But Jesus recognized his deepest need and took care of that one first.

In a similar vein, you may have people in your life who don't want—or think they need—forgiveness. But by showing forgiveness and mercy toward them, you just might rock their world. Yours too.

(By the way, if you're thinking, "Hey, I bet a skunk would make a cool pet," take it from Todd. Go with a goldfish instead.)

SLICE OF ADVICE:

"Therefore, rid yourselves of all malice" (1 Peter 2:1). Note how the verse says "all" malice. This is one of the reasons we love the Bible. In an age of relativism and equivocation and disclaimers (Void Where Prohibited, Limited Warranty, Certain Restrictions May Apply, etc.), it's one place you can turn for a pure, straightforward position on something.

 **DELIVER ON THIS:**

Chances are, you probably have a grudge against someone in your life. Be honest with yourself. Take a big whiff. Can you smell even a faint stench of bitterness? Is it coming from you? If this is the case, it's time to set yourself free of what is dragging you down, eating away at your insides, polluting your perception of the world. It's time to forgive and move on.

How do you do this? Relax, you don't have to find your arch-nemesis, place your benevolent hand on his forehead, and proclaim, "I forgive thee, my brother." That's not going to help. Instead, what you need to do is say good-bye to the hateful, resentful thoughts. Stop with the evil-eye glances and cold tone of voice. Stop bad-mouthing this person to your friends. Stop with the inner celebrations every time he or she fails at something. Pray that God will help you find a place of peace with this person. This doesn't mean you have to become best buds. And it doesn't mean that you start telling a blabbermouth all of your most personal secrets. God wants us to be forgiving; he doesn't require us to be foolish.

What it does mean is taking every action—and ceasing every reaction—until every scrap of malice has been swept from your heart. You'll feel better—we promise. So go get a broom.

ADVENTURES WITH TOOTHPASTE

o say that we Hafer brothers are accident-prone is like saying that the sun is "rising-prone." We bump into things. We misplace things. And we spill things. Fortunately, we are usually able to rectify our mistakes. Bruises—wrought by evil coffee tables with sharp corners—eventually heal. Cheap sunglasses left on top of the car can be replaced for seven bucks at the grocery store. And even Fruity Pebbles, poured with the best of intentions for one of our younger kids, can be swept back into the box when we somehow miss the bowl.

However, we recently discovered a spillage situation that is without remedy. If you squeeze a stubborn tube of toothpaste from the middle and a "toothpaste snake" thirteen inches long accidentally squirts out, there is no going back. No amount of strategic pulling and prodding on the tube will coax that toothpaste back into its home. Once it's out, it's *out.*

This toothpaste mishap got us thinking about words—not merely because both have to do with the mouth. Words, like toothpaste, are irrevocable. Now, you may remember a scene from your childhood in which someone said something mean to you and you grabbed this kid, threw him to the ground, sat on his stomach and demanded, "You take that back!"

To get you off his stomach, this person (perhaps he was a brother, right, Jedd?) might have conceded. "Okay, okay, I take it back. Just get offa me!"

But this concession was only symbolic. The words were out there; the damage was done.

You know where we're going with this. You need to choose your words carefully because they are unretractable and they have power. Really. They can make a difference, for good or for harm.

We have discovered this truth, as we try to encourage people—on the job and on speaking tours. People hunger for kind words the way a marathon finisher thirsts for a cup of cold water. The way some people smile and blush, we wonder how long it's been since someone complimented them.

And you don't have to be popular, well-known, or successful for a compliment to make a difference. (We know, because we aren't well-known, popular, or successful.) And yet, when we asked Tricia Brock from Superchic(k) to write the foreword for one of our books, she said she was "really honored." We couldn't believe it. Superchic(k) is one of our favorite bands. They can fill huge auditoriums. Tricia herself has been named one of the most influential young artists in Christian music.

And yet, for some reason, it touched her that we wanted her to be associated with one of our books. The same is true of Nichole Nordeman, who has won Dove Awards in all the major categories and has massive talent as a songwriter and singer. She penned the foreword for another of our books and told us that it meant a lot to her that we asked her for the favor.

Words can work the other way too. We met a guy who was ridiculed by peers in his vocal group for a solo part that didn't go well. Their words stung so deeply that he didn't sing in public again for years.

Philip Yancey, one of our favorite writers, was called "the slow one" by his mother, because as a child he didn't seem to be as bright as his older brother. It took years before he was able to rise above the label. He's now known as one of the sharpest minds in Christendom.

What you say matters. Words make an immediate impact. Words make a lasting impact. We urge you to be a source of words that heal, not wound; inspire, not discourage; comfort, not irritate; build up, not tear down.

 ## SLICE OF ADVICE:

"Pleasant words are as an honeycomb, sweet to the soul, and health to the bones" (Proverbs 16:24 KJV).

 ## DELIVER ON THIS:

Remember that toothpaste analogy at the beginning of this devo? Here's one more reason we used it: We trust that you are practicing good oral hygiene. (You are, right? *Right?*) If that is the case, you should be brushing your teeth at least before you go to bed at night. So here's your assignment, every time you brush your teeth, make it a habit to do a "word inventory." Let before-bed brushing time also be a time for taking stock of how you used words during the day. Did you, as the Bible urges, "speak the truth in love"?

If you are also a morning brusher—and good for you if you are—you can let this time remind you to choose your words carefully during the day ahead. We know this particular "Deliver on This" is a real mouthful, but you can handle it. Okay, now rinse and spit.

GARBAGE IN, GARBAGE OUT

aybe you've seen the movie *Supersize Me* or read the book about the guy who ate only fast food for a month—and how it messed up his body big-time. It was scary stuff.

Now, don't worry. We're not going to use this chapter to harsh on America's fast-food outlets. We eat at those places sometimes. There, we admit it. Let him who is without the occasional late-night craving for a McDonald's #7 meal cast the first French fry.

Still, this guy's little experiment hit us hard. Sure, we've all heard the phrase "Garbage in, garbage out." But do we really take the time to examine and consider how we feed our hearts and minds—and how that kind of "junk food" affects us?

Just like a computer, the information we feed ourselves helps determine what comes out. There is no denying that our hearts and attitudes are shaped by what we see, hear, and experience daily. If we take in violence, messages of sexual immorality, messages that dishonor the Living God and devalue his people, we *will* be affected. We aren't immune. Otherwise, why would companies spend billions of dollars producing print and electronic ads designed to get us to consume? Why would the music business spend millions of dollars producing videos, if not to sell records?

Of course, listening to one negative song or seeing one violent movie will not turn you into a serial murderer. For that reason, many Christian young people conclude, "I can handle this stuff. I've seen worse. No harm," then proceed to exercise zero caution or judgment.

Even Christian parents assume, "My kid is mature. My kid has a strong foundation. He/she can handle intense stuff." And with that, they cease to regulate what their kids take into their minds and hearts.

Your body can "handle" a certain amount of toxic material. For example, did you know that apple seeds contain a small amount of poison? You could eat one—even a few—with little or no side effects. But eat a cupful or two in one sitting and it could kill you. In the same way, if you happen to be at a party and inadvertently see a few seconds of an ultra-violent movie or video game, or a sex scene, it probably won't traumatize you or scar you for life. But sit down and get comfortable with stuff like that, and it might start to change you. It might make you hungry for more.

Be wary of cumulative effects. Spiritual junk food, spiritual toxic waste, can build up and produce harmful consequences. Let's go back to the example from the first paragraph. The subject of the *Supersize* movie didn't get nauseated after his first burger. He didn't start feeling depressed or experiencing sexual dysfunction after his first snack of French fries with a chocolate-shake chaser. But over time, he suffered from these symptoms—and more. And remember, this was just a month-long experiment.

The same kind of phenomenon can happen if you feed your brain, your spirit, too much junk. Watching pornography—or even the way network TV cheapens human physical intimacy—can warp the way you perceive sexuality. We find it heartbreaking that the people who make the "Girls Gone Wild" and "Guys Gone Wild" videos can find so many willing participants—and eager consumers. We're going to go out on a limb here and hypothesize that this kind of thing does NOT represent God's ideal for human sexuality.

Let's move on now and talk about sex's longtime media partner, violence. We have become desensitized to violence and death. Stuff that would literally have made our grandparents shudder—or maybe even vomit—barely makes us blink. Think about how many people you have seen get blown away in movies, TV shows, or video games. We've seen a lot too. We didn't realize how much this exposure affected us until we had to sit and hold a real person's hand while she died or stand and stare in stunned disbelief at a longtime friend lying lifeless in a coffin.

You see, in the real world, death is profound, and it shakes you to your core. People matter. Their passing from this world is far from insignificant. But that is usually not the message you glean from the media.

With apologies to our gamer friends out there, we need to point out that we find violent video games especially concerning because they are so effective in hardening our hearts to violence.

Think about it: If you see somebody get blown away in a movie, you might feel bad—if it's a hero, not a villain. You might feel empathy and think, "How terrible! That poor person!" But chances are that if *you* blow somebody away in a video game, you're going to be *happy* about it! You are practicing to kill without remorse—to cease valuing life and to act violently without hesitating or considering consequences. That is why police and military use simulators for conflict situations; it makes it easier to handle the real thing!

And we won't soon forget the quotes from Eric Harris and Dylan Klebold, the killers who massacred classmates and a teacher at Columbine High School. As they looked forward to their bloody rampage, they said gleefully, "It's gonna be like [the video game] 'Doom,' man!" We grew up near Columbine High School. We personally know kids who were affected by what happened there on April 20, 1999. We walked the school grounds days after the tragedy. We saw victims' cars, still in their parking places. Only now, students had transformed them into memorials to their fallen classmates. We saw students and parents in clusters, hugging each other and crying. What happened at Columbine was no game.

At this point, we must note that we don't blame "the media" for the world's problems. We don't think that most people will be turned into violent criminals or sex fiends simply because of the media they experience. (We believe the media can be contributing factors with some people, because we have seen it happen.)

But, most likely, you aren't going to be transformed into something evil by a CD or a video game. Our message here still applies: Don't let electronic junk food dominate your media diet. "Give me one good reason," you might argue. How about *three* good reasons?

1. The Bible commands us to make the most of our time. We aren't saying that all of your free time should be spent studying Deuteronomy and writing psalms. We recognize the need for entertainment. Pure entertainment. Escapism. We simply ask you to ask yourself this question as you make entertainment choices: Is this a wise use of my time and money?

2. You might feel you are immune to some of the lies portrayed by certain media, such as "Casual sex is fun, and you'll never have to worry about pregnancy or AIDS." "Drunk people are hilarious and fun to be around." "It's all about *you*." "If somebody crosses you, blow 'em away!" "If you drink and party, you'll be surrounded by hot members of the opposite sex—and maybe a pirate and a performing dog to boot!" Maybe you are strong, but over time your resistance can be worn down. Don't believe us? Ever caught yourself singing along to a song on the radio and realized that the lyrics are incredibly offensive? Not long ago, Todd was driving members of a preteen girls' basketball team to get a snack and had to turn off the radio when he heard them singing, "I'm into having sex—I ain't into makin' love." Now, we're not saying that a few lyrics from 50 Cent are going to drive an SUV-load of innocent girls into promiscuity, but no one will ever be able to convince us that it's harmless for young girls to be happily singing lyrics like this. That is, plain and simple, messed up.

There is a reason that God commands us to guard our hearts and minds.

3. Your entertainment choices are helping somebody make money, so you need to decide what kind of people and what kind of media you want to support. If your favorite artist brags about how much Jack Daniel's he drinks or how much pot he smokes, guess where at least some of your concert-ticket, CD, or DVD dollars are going?

Similarly, if you keep buying DVDs featuring drunken college students debasing themselves, people will keep making more of them. If you help make *Naked Drunken Road Trip* a box-office smash, you will help bring about *Naked Drunken Road Trip 2* and *Naked Drunken Road Trip 3: In 3-D!*

We can largely control what we put into our computers—our minds and hearts. Gods says to feed ourselves a steady diet of whatever is excellent, pure, lovely, true, noble, right, and praiseworthy. Focus on good input, he commands, and you'll get good output.

One final note here: We don't tout the philosophy that says "Christian media, good; secular media, *bad.*" We urge you to hold all media to the standard in the paragraph above. "Christian" does not always equal "excellent." Now, it's unlikely that you are going to find a Christian book or movie or song that is gratuitously violent or sexually impure. But you might find pathetic acting, derivative lyrics, or a holy mystery reduced to a rip-off of a beer-commercial slogan. Hey, we are part of Christian media, but we have to be honest and note that our industry has produced enough cheesy material to make nachos for the entire world.

So we urge you to make wise choices with all your entertainment options. Slapping a Christian label on something doesn't make it excellent or worthy of your time or money.

DOUBLE SLICE OF ADVICE:

1. The time you kill feeding on mental and spiritual junk food can never be resuscitated.

2. Guarding your heart and your mind shows respect for the One who gave them to you.

DELIVER ON THIS:

As you evaluate your entertainment choices, put everything through the Philippians 4:8 test—Christian *and* mainstream stuff. Here are those criteria one more time:

Excellent
Pure
Lovely
True
Noble
Right
Praiseworthy
Admirable

REGULATING PEER PRESSURE

F ew of life's choices are as significant as your choice of friends. That was a rather easy sentence to write, but it's a tough one to live out. First of all, even the term "choice of friends" is troubling. Do we really "choose" our friends, or does friendship just seem to happen?

Few of us remember going up to a prospective friend and saying, "Okay, I pick you—aren't you lucky?"

However, while friendships do have a way of "just happening," there is an element of choice involved. You might feel that fate brought you and your close friends together, but it will take more than something as nebulous as "fate" to keep you together. And in some cases you might find that you need to end a friendship, or at least place limits on it.

This brings us to what many people see as a contradiction in the Christian life. Jesus befriended all kinds of people, many of them criminals and social outcasts. Christians are supposed to follow Jesus as the supreme example. And yet, when we read the Bible, we find verses like "He who walks with the wise grows wise, but a companion of fools suffers harm" (Proverbs 13:20).

How do we solve this dilemma? How do we follow Jesus' example *and* protect ourselves from harm?

Here are a few guidelines that have helped us—and brought us trouble when we neglected to take our own advice:

1. Follow Jesus' *complete* example. Yes, Jesus befriended the ragamuffins of the world, but note how he always maintained control of those relationships. He was a leader, not a follower. He kept control of the situation. Remember how some of his friends wanted to turn him into a political leader, yet he resisted? He knew his purpose in life, and he didn't let anyone—even his friends—distract him.

2. Constantly monitor your friendships, especially those involving people who like to dance with danger. You must ask yourself regularly, "Am I drawing this person closer to God, or is he or she hampering my relationship with my Creator—drawing me away?" "Is this friendship putting me into compromising situations—such as in a car with people who are drinking or at a party where there are drugs, alcohol, or guns?"

3. Don't abandon your friendships with solid Christian people so you can spend all of your time with the people you are trying to help. You need your Christian friends to keep you accountable, offer advice and support, and pray for you and with you.

4. Don't compromise your standards in order to be accepted by a non-Christian friend—or that friend's peers. For example, did you know that, according to the U.S. Department of Health, kids who have three or more friends who smoke are ten times more likely to smoke than those who report that none of their friends smoke?

   Look at it this way: You are accepting a friend even though he or she doesn't share your beliefs. You aren't demanding, "Become something you are not, or I won't be your friend." You have the right to expect the same kind of acceptance from your wilder breed of friends. You don't require that people become Christians to associate with you; they shouldn't expect you to check your Christianity at the door before they'll let you into their lives.

You can influence your non-Christian friends for good (and we mean "for good" in more ways than one). The key is to be discerning and watchful. We know that this is a challenge; we face it every day. We hope the "friendly" advice we've offered will help you.

 **SLICE OF ADVICE:**

"Dear friend, if bad companions tempt you, don't go along with them" (Proverbs 1:10 MESSAGE).

 **DELIVER ON THIS:**

As you walk that precarious tightrope called friendship, use the guidelines above as a checklist. They have really helped us and continue to do so. Friendship can be complex, mysterious, and confusing. Powerful emotions are involved, sometimes *conflicting* powerful emotions. That is why it's useful to have set guidelines in place.

PARENTS: HONOR AND OBEY?

Bad news—we don't get to choose our parents. Good news—somebody much wiser than we are chose them for us.

Relationships with moms and dads provide the closest model of humanity's relationship with God.

As much as we hate to admit the need to obey, God has designed a system for our protection. In general, when we obey God (and, in most cases, our parents), we are protected. On the other hand, when we rebel, we go outside that protection and we put ourselves in dangerous positions.

You can watch this phenomenon with little kids. They venture out and test things, often going for the most dangerous options first. Imagine a two-year-old left unsupervised in the world for any length of time. He or she would be in deep trouble in a hurry. That's why a parent must constantly intervene to set limits and keep kids safe.

Recently, we've seen some of the videotaped studies in which researchers placed a real gun (unloaded) among a bunch of toys in the middle of a preschool playroom. The kids were drawn like magnets to the gun.

It's easy to see how we need parental protection when we are little. But we also continue to need rules, limits, guidance, and even discipline as we get older. And despite all the other influences in a young person's life, parents still top the list, according to Lawrence Kutner, a child psychologist and teacher.

With all due respect, a sixteen-year-old, alone and unchecked in the world, can get into deep trouble pretty quickly too. Sure, we are wiser at sixteen, but we are not bulletproof or immortal. In fact, the worst trouble the Hafer brothers got into came when our parents let us have too much freedom.

Not only do we need the authority and guidance, but we also need the closeness and the relationship a parent can provide. We need to be able to talk with the adults in our lives.

God put these people in your life for a reason. You can learn from them. And it's your duty to show them love and honor—even when you feel they don't deserve it.

We hear parenting experts all the time telling moms and dads they need to get involved in their kids' lives, to learn about their interests and meet them on their level.

As good as this advice may be for adults, consider the fact that sons and daughters have a responsibility to do the same. Now, we understand that some of you might have parents who are alcoholic, disconnected, irresponsible. You might feel that they don't deserve your respect and obedience. You might be right. But we urge you to strive to be respectful and obedient anyway. You won't change a parent's attitude or behavior by being defiant any more than you'll change the speed limit in your neighborhood by breaking it constantly. Conversely, think about the impression you might be able to make when you show respect and obedience that *isn't* deserved.

You might have asked yourself, "Why did God allow me to have the parents (or stepparents) that I am stuck with? They aren't having a positive impact on my life." This is a great question, a completely legit question. We don't know if we have an answer for you. Still, we might. Could it be that God brought the cold and distant stepfather or short-tempered mother into your life not for the ways that they'll enhance your life, but for the ways that you will change *them*?

Also, it could be that destructive patterns you see in your parents have been passed down through generations. Maybe you can be one to finally break the cycle—to learn from the mistakes of previous generations and establish a new standard.

Whatever your situation, being genuinely respectful, thoughtful, and obedient will be your best course of action. This approach can make a strong parent/teen relationship even stronger—and a rocky relationship at least a little smoother.

 **SLICE OF ADVICE:**

"Children obey your parents in all things, for this is well-pleasing to the Lord" (Colossians 3:20 NKJV).

PLEASE, EASY ON THE CHEESE

You might hear your peers say, "Why should we listen to our parents? They are far from perfect, and they don't understand what it's like to be a teen. Why should we listen to people who make just as many mistakes as we do—if not more?"

This is flawed logic—and an excuse not to listen. You don't have to be perfect to recognize a problem and give sound advice for correcting it. The very fact that parents aren't perfect can help them give road-tested advice. In most cases, parents *know* they aren't perfect—and they want to help their kids avoid the mistakes they have made themselves.

Finally, if it weren't important for us to respect and obey our parents, God wouldn't have commanded it.

 **DELIVER ON THIS:**

Be a student—and a fan—of your parents. Your challenge is not only to obey but also to seek out ways to honor and thank mom and/or dad. This might be as simple as doing what you are asked the first time—and without rolling your eyes and sighing heavily.

LET'S ERASE RACISM!

I *am not nor have I ever been in favor of making voters or jurors of Negroes, nor of qualifying them to hold office, nor to intermarry with white people. . . . There is a physical difference between the white and black races which I believe will forever forbid the two races living together on terms of social and political equality."*

Who do you think uttered those words? Adolph Hitler? A Grand Wizard of the Ku Klux Klan?

How about Abraham Lincoln? That's right. That's a direct quote from Honest Abe, the great Emancipator himself. And he wasn't uneducated, politically ignorant, or devoid of life experience when he uttered them. He was a lawyer and a national spokesman for the Republican Party, with an eye on the presidency of the United States.

In time, however, Lincoln's views changed. Maybe it was the courage and intelligence he saw two hundred thousand African Americans display in battle during the Civil War. Perhaps the God he so often spoke of changed his mind and heart. Whatever the case, just four years after issuing this racist statement, President Lincoln issued the Emancipation Proclamation, clearing the path for the Thirteenth Amendment, which ended slavery in the U.S.

Unfortunately, no one has been able to draft an amendment to end distrust, hatred, and bigotry among different races. And if even one of history's finest men wasn't immune from racist views, is it any wonder that this problem still exists today? From the basketball court to corporate boardrooms, people today still try to separate and divide people on the basis of their color.

Sadly, some Christians try to use the Bible to justify their prejudice. They make references to slavery in biblical times or misappropriate verses about "light not having anything in common with darkness." It's reality-check time: God sees only one race: the human one. And the Bible couldn't be more plain: "There is neither Jew nor Greek, slave nor free, male nor female, for you are all one in Christ Jesus" (Galatians 3:28).

Anyone who tries to justify racism using the Bible is twisting the message and the spirit of God's Word. Yes, Jesus did wear a white robe. It didn't have a matching hood. Jesus prayed fervently to God the Father that all believers would "be brought to complete unity to let the world know that you sent me. . . ." (John 17:23). Think about that: Unity among believers is a sign to the world that Jesus was truly commissioned by God.

Imagine, then, what our Creator thinks when some of his creation think they are better than others simply because of the tone of their skin. This is pure ignorance and pride. And it is learned. We remember well taking our toddlers to playgrounds where they encountered Asian kids, Hispanic kids, and African-American kids. They all played together, with no fear, no prejudice, no suspicion, no mistrust. They weren't threatened by the differences in skin tone. Occasionally, they would bring one of their playmates over to introduce him or her to us. And they never said, "This is my friend with light brown skin" or "This is my friend with curly hair and dark brown skin." They simply said, with joy in their voices, "Here's my new friend!"

This brings us to our challenge to you. We urge you to discover the joy—and promote the healing—that can be found in reaching out to and befriending people who don't look like you.

We've found that today's teens are doing more to promote racial harmony than their older counterparts. Keep it up. Pray every day for racial harmony. Pursue relationships with people of different ethnicities. Enjoy the beauty of diversity. As you do these things, you will help bring about an answer to Jesus' prayer in John 17. (How cool is *that*?) And you can be sure that the heart of God, the creative artist who plays no favorites, will be with you.

 **SLICE OF ADVICE:**

"We must learn to live together like brothers or we will perish together like fools." Martin Luther King Jr.

 **DELIVER ON THIS:**

Is there a person in your life—someone who doesn't look like you—that you can reach out to, befriend, defend, learn from? Chances are there is someone like this. And chances are you know how to engage this person. So what are you waiting for?

YOUR ACTIONS LEAD BETTER THAN WORDS

T his chapter is especially for you if you are a young leader. Maybe you're a captain of a sports team. Maybe you help out in Sunday school or serve with an organization like Big Brothers or Big Sisters or baby-sit for neighbors. You could be a biological big brother or big sister—or just someone that your peer group looks to as a leader.

We know that leadership is hard. Sometimes it helps to have an example to follow. We're going to give you two.

John Wooden is a college basketball legend. During his years as head coach at UCLA, his teams won a host of national titles. Losses were rare for Wooden's Bruins, and he coached many players, including Bill Walton and Kareem Abdul-Jabbar, who went on to be superstars in the NBA.

Many factors contributed to Wooden's success. He was a student of the game. He had an eye for talent. He was a great motivator.

However, when former players talk about the privilege of playing for Coach Wooden, they reveal the true key to his effectiveness as a leader:

He led by example. One of his most famous axioms was, "I never ask a player to do anything—during a game or in practice—that I haven't done myself." Because of this, Coach Wooden's players knew that any drills he put them through were for their benefit and he really wasn't asking them to do something impossible or difficult to the point of being cruel.

Additionally, Wooden didn't order his players to maintain their composure during games while he screamed at officials, threw chairs, or manhandled a confused point guard (as other famous college coaches have been known to do). Wooden was an intense competitor, but he didn't let his intensity make him do something foolish that would embarrass him or cost his team a game.

Wooden had a kindred spirit who lived two hundred years before he did. Ben Franklin was another wise man who understood that an ounce of leading by example was worth ten pounds of leading by pressure and intimidation. For example, at one point in his life, Franklin wanted his city, Philadelphia, to lighten up. He believed that lighting the city's streets would not only improve it aesthetically but also make it safer. But he didn't try to persuade Philly's citizens by talking to them. Instead, he hung a beautiful lantern near his front door. He kept the lantern brightly polished and carefully and faithfully lit the wick each evening just before dusk.

People strolling the dark street saw Franklin's light from a long way off. They found its glow to be friendly and beautiful—and a helpful, guiding landmark. Soon, Franklin's neighbors began placing lanterns in front of their own homes. Before long, the whole city was dotted with light, and more and more people began to appreciate the beauty and value of Franklin's bright idea.

Lighting the streets became a city-wide—and city-sponsored—endeavor.

Just as Franklin became a point of light for his city, our actions can become beacons for those around us—friends, siblings, teammates, fellow youth-group members, and so on. What they see, they copy. And when they see the light of your good example, they may be inspired to illuminate a candle of their own.

SLICE OF ADVICE:

People may doubt what you say, but they will always believe what you do.

DELIVER ON THIS:

Think about a specific action or behavior you want to model for someone who looks up to you as a leader. Now brainstorm ways that you can lead by example. Having these ideas in your head will help you be a more effective role model. For example, if you have a younger sibling who is starting to pepper his or her speech with profanities, commit to expressing yourself—especially in volatile situations—without resorting to a string of expletives. This will help you keep your tongue in check and set a positive example.

DRUGS: WHO'S DOING WHOM?

None of us are without struggle. None of us have gone through life without blowing it in a major way. Some sins and struggles are more obvious, more dangerous, than others.

One of the greatest honors we've experienced has been the chance to share in the serious struggles and triumphs of real people. It's so awesome to know real people who have been down tough roads and are willing to honestly share how they have overcome huge challenges.

You are about to meet one of those awesome individuals. His name is Terrence, and the interview below, we hope, will change the way you think about drugs.

Q: *You were once addicted to drugs. You compared that experience to "falling down a hole." How far did you fall, and how fast?*

A: Farther than I ever thought I could. So fast that I didn't even realize I was falling. One minute I was at a party, listening to some music with a few new friends; the next minute I was desperate—doing things I never thought I'd do in a million years—all for the next high. I became such a slave. There was no hideous thing I wouldn't do. Within weeks, I hated drugs. I hated getting high, but I *had* to.

Q: *What was drug addiction like?*

A: It was like a trap, and I felt so stupid because I walked into it willingly. I wasn't stupid. I was a smart kid. I knew the dangers. All these politicians keep talking about education—kids need to be told that drugs are bad. That's weak. Kids *know* drugs are bad for them. I knew, but I chose them anyway. I thought, "Other guys can't handle it, but I'm smart. I'm strong. I can stop. I'll be careful. I'll be able to control it." And then, as soon as I started using, I knew I'd been taken. It was such a lie, but it was too late.

Q: *Tell us more about the illusion of control.*

A: Like you said, it's an illusion. I wasn't doing the drugs; they were doing me. I never really had control from the moment I chose to step over the line and get messed up for the first time. You don't want to panic, so you tell yourself, "It's cool. This isn't so bad. I'm just like all these other people." But the truth is that you're dying and you know it, like, ten seconds after you start. And that's about nine seconds too late. It's like those bad horror movies where the girl's walking around in the dark. You hear the scary music playing and you know she's going to get killed in some gruesome way—but you just keep watching, helplessly, as she just keeps stepping closer to danger.

Q: *As a drug user, are you the victim or the one watching the movie?*

A: You're both of them. You're the girl because you're stupid and you shouldn't be there in the first place. You should get out of there and get back to safety. You're also the viewer because you're helpless to do anything. You can't stop it. You might as well be watching yourself walking stupidly to your own death. You can't turn it off even though you know how it's going to end.

Q: *How did you stop doing drugs?*

A: I didn't just stop doing drugs. I became a new person. I'm still becoming that person every day, actually. I can't stop running in the opposite direction from [drugs] or it just might catch me. God has helped me a lot to change my identity. I said I was a Christian before I got into drugs, but I wasn't living it. I wasn't a new creation. I'd say to anyone out there, if you have an addiction or a bad habit, don't just stop that behavior; change your whole identity. Become somebody else—someone who would never do the destructive things you are doing. Change your friends if they're into drugs. I did. I changed jobs, locations, habits, my thinking, the way I talked and dressed. Anything that fed my old ways. If I went back to my old hangouts, parties, or same group of friends, I'd be [under the influence] right now.

Q: *Is there anything else you'd like to say to the readers of this book?*

A: All my old friends make fun of that "Just Say No" slogan. But I'll tell you, that's good advice. Don't even *start* going down that road. It's really hard to turn back.

SLICE OF ADVICE:

Don't let the pursuit of a "good time" separate you from the One who loves you. It will only leave you empty and broken. Don't let drugs drag you down.

PLEASE, EASY ON THE CHEESE

You might hear the argument, "How can you dis drugs before you've even tried them? Come on, once isn't going to hurt you." We wanted to grill this cheese, but we decided to let

Terrence do it: "I thought just one little time wouldn't hurt. That one time led to thousands of wasted dollars, one hospitalization, almost dying, and years of regret. Won't *hurt*? I have just one word for you . . . OUCH!"

 **DELIVER ON THIS:**

Listen to the voice of experience. Make a promise to God right now that you will never (or never again) defile the mind and body he gave you with drugs.

VIRGINS REVISITED

O kay, it's confession time again. The Hafer brothers tend to over-commit themselves. With the speaking gigs, the writing gigs, the "real jobs," parenting, church-league hoops, and so on, we often find ourselves frozen in the headlights of a fast-approaching dead-line. Thank heaven for merciful publishers who are usually gracious enough to extend deadlines for us—even if it delays the release of a book.

However, sometimes the extra writing time provides an unexpected fringe benefit. It took us so long to finish this book, for example, those virgins we interviewed earlier in the book had time to get married! (They all had serious boyfriends during the first interviews, okay? It didn't take us *that* long to finish the book!) This afforded us a great opportunity to conduct follow-up interviews and find out if "waiting" was really worth it. What follows is a composite of conversations with three very happy—and perfectly legit—"no-longer-virgins."

Q: *While you were striving to keep yourself pure, many of your* *peers caved in to sexual temptation. How and why did this happen?*

Laura: A lot of my friends were in relationships that they thought would be long-term, so that's how they rationalized having sex. I also have friends who were abused, and that affected their sense of self-worth. They accepted that their "role" was to be used sexually. Others were looking for love to cover up the hurt. In both cases, they resorted to sex for the wrong reasons.

Q: *Are any of your friends with their sexual partners from their teen years?*

Vickie: No. You change so much during your teen years—and after that too. That's why I encourage teens I talk with to stay strong. When you are a teen, you are still finding who you are. You don't know what you'll be like in a few years, and you don't know what your boyfriend or girlfriend will be like. I know that, for me, my idea of the kind of guy I wanted to spend my life with changed dramatically after I left my teen years behind.

Q: *You have married friends who didn't stay pure as teens; how do they feel about that now?*

Vickie: So many of my friends have expressed regret to me. They feel guilty. And they feel bad about their spouses' sexual past as well. One of my friends held to the standard, but her husband didn't. He didn't tell her about his past until after they were engaged. She felt so bad that she wouldn't be able to be her husband's "first." She had all these insecurities—about disease, would her husband be comparing her to his previous partners—that kind of thing.

Q: *Even with the specter of STDs and pregnancy always looming, teens still decide to have sex. Any explanation?*

Andi: In your teen years, you feel indestructible. You don't think "it" can happen to you. I work in the medical profession now, and one of the things they teach you about dealing with death, for example, is that young children actually cope with it much better than teens do—when a parent, sibling, or peer dies. I've seen that "wall of indestructibility" come down in other ways too. When a sexually active teen comes into the hospital with certain symptoms—such as abdominal pains—all of these worries start popping up: "Am I pregnant?" "Do I have an STD?" "If I do have an STD, is it AIDS—am I going to die?" Sexual promiscuity adds so much worry to life; it's sad that too many teens don't realize that sooner.

Q: *You are married now. What would you say to teens who are finding it difficult to hold on to their purity?*

Vickie: It's worth it to stay a virgin until you are married. It's more than worth it. I knew God would reward me for obeying him, but the reward was greater than I ever imagined. I'm not saying that people who make a mistake can't find grace and forgiveness and have a fulfilling marriage, but it makes it so much sweeter if you wait. I am thankful that my husband and I didn't drag any sexual baggage into our relationship. It made things more intimate. The Bible talks about a man and a woman becoming "one flesh," a oneness that is emotional, physical, and spiritual. Think about it—how can you become "one" with a bunch of different people?

Laura: If you are staying pure, you are not missing out on anything. You are ensuring your future happiness.

SLICE OF ADVICE:

Waiting is worth it. You won't regret it. Just ask a virgin on his or her honeymoon.

 ## DELIVER ON THIS:

Here's an assignment for you: Conduct your own "former virgin" interview. Find someone—or even a couple—who stayed pure until marriage. Ask questions about how they did it—actually, *didn't* do it—and the rewards they enjoyed as a result.

TIME TO REHEAT IT

Here are a few thoughts worth plucking from the fridge and warming up. . . .

1. You need to think and talk about sex *more*, not less. Just make sure you speak and think wisely and purely.

2. Remember, you can learn more from asking and pondering questions than from being spoon-fed answers.

3. Know how good it feels to be forgiven? It feels just as good to forgive. So forgive someone.

4. Your words have power. It's your choice whether the power will be to build up or to tear down.

5. Garbage in, garbage out. It applies to computers, the human body, and, most important, hearts and minds. What are you feeding yours?

6. Are you drawing your friends closer to God, or are they yanking you away from him? If the latter is the case, you need to pull harder—or cut the rope.

7. Whether your parents are wonderful or wack, showing them respect will make your life, and theirs, better.

8. Want to be a leader? Lead by action. People may doubt what you say, but they will always believe what you do.

9. Here's the truth about drugs: You don't do them; *they do you.* (Note how both our drug-free and drug-damaged interviewees used that same wording?) And drugs don't just do you; they might just do you in.

10. One hundred percent of virgins surveyed said staying pure until marriage was well worth the wait.

BECOME A FREESTYLE FLEEING CHAMPION!

I magine that you are walking down a dark alley and a machete-wielding madman pops out from behind a Dumpster and charges at you. Or as you're going for a run, you look over your shoulder and see a pack of rabid Rottweilers closing in on you, snarling and snapping their foam-flecked jaws. Would anyone have to tell you to flee?

Sadly, we regularly encounter something much more dangerous than a crazed criminal or canine—and we keep walking right toward it. We are talking about temptation. Temptation that is custom-designed to capitalize on our weaknesses. (That's how the forces of evil work; the Bible defines Satan as a schemer and a liar. If you are an avowed vegan who becomes nauseated at the mere mention of the word "meat," Satan will not try to tempt you by waving steak tartare under your nose and chanting, "Beef—it's what's for dinner, and lunch, and breakfast!")

Remember when Jesus was alone and hungry in the wilderness? That's when Satan pounced—when he thought his prey would be vulnerable. And how did Satan try to tempt him? With food. With power.

With a test that angels would come to his aid in his time of peril.

We need to recognize temptation for what it is—an evil attempt to destroy us and allow the forces of evil to sneer at God as they damage and deceive yet another of the children that he loves. If temptation is a dog, it will come to you, not as the ferocious Rottweiler, but as a cute, eager puppy begging for your attention.

Fortunately, God has provided a way out: Flee! This is hard advice for a marathon runner like Todd to endorse, but in this case, even he will acknowledge that when temptation is charging at you, it's time to forget about warming up, stretching, and running an even pace. Just run like mad. Don't look back. Our bud Steven Curtis Chapman says it well: "Don't even look in the direction of a thought you should not entertain."

What makes SC²'s advice so apt is that if we start entertaining the thought, that thought will pull up a chair and want to hang with us for a long time. We'll stop listening to the voice of godly reason and start listening to the lies and half-truths and rationalizations: "Burning one blunt isn't going to kill anybody." "Okay, I have to lie to get myself out of this mess, but this is the *last* time." "What happens on spring break *stays* on spring break."

How do we find the willpower to flee in the face of these enticing lies? Jesus provides our example. Remember the satanic temptation we noted above? Jesus first recognized the temptation for what it was. For example, when Satan tried to get him to turn stones into bread, he knew that his enemy wasn't concerned for his physical well-being. He knew it was an attempt to manipulate him, entice him to break his fast.

The other important example that Jesus set was to use truth from the Bible—truth in context—to refute Satan's attempts to twist Scripture. Satan tried to get Jesus to do a swan dive off the pinnacle of a temple. "The angels will catch you," he said. "The Bible says so." Jesus replied, "You shall not tempt the Lord your God."

You can do the same thing. You can recognize temptation for what it is. You can use the Bible to gain the wisdom and the strength to turn and flee. God promises that we will never be tested beyond what we can bear. This is because he loves us.

We put this temptation chapter after the "former virgin" chapter for a reason. Those ex-virgins we interviewed all faced temptation. They all had plenty of dates and had serious, long-term relationships before they got married. But they all trusted God's promise that they would be able to withstand temptation, and they knew they would be rewarded for their obedience.

We hope their story will help you recognize that God's rules for living are for your protection—and to ensure your long-term, guilt-free enjoyment of life.

DOUBLE SLICE OF ADVICE:

1. "Therefore submit to God. Resist the devil" (James 4:7 NKJV).
2. "Blessed is the man who endures temptation; for when he has been approved, he will receive the crown of life which the Lord has promised to those who love Him" (James 1:12 NKJV).

DELIVER ON THIS:

Take time right now to determine your weakest point, your biggest temptation. (This might take only a couple of seconds—a lot of us know exactly where we are most vulnerable.) It might be pornography, dishonesty, a violent temper, drugs or alcohol, sexual activity. It is vital to admit your weakness; this is no time for denial.

Identifying this "Achilles' heel" is an important first step—awareness. But you need to be more than aware—you need to be prepared. You need to understand that this weak point is going to be attacked, but it probably won't be a full-frontal attack. So watch your flanks, watch your back. Watch for temptations disguised as harmless activities, friends disguised as enemies. Become the master of the quick exit, the daring escape. Become a freestyle fleeing champion.

TIME TO TAKE A JOY RIDE

Who are the happiest people you know? Are *you* one of the happiest people you know? This is a question we posed to friends, relatives, co-workers—anyone who would talk to us. (People who were scowling were not queried, as we deemed them to be either angry, grumpy, or constipated.) Then we hit 'em with this follow-up: What makes happy people so joyful? A variety of answers tumbled out, but after studying them for a while, we found some common elements—seven of them, in fact. This made us happy, because seven is a good biblical number. So here they are—the Hafer Brothers' Happy Super Seven:

1. Happy people are often parents, big brothers and big sisters, grandparents, teachers, Sunday school leaders, and others who spend their time pouring their lives into those of others—especially younger people.

2. Happy people don't live in the best circumstances. Very few are wealthy (financially at least). Many are not young and/or

in excellent physical health. Almost none are famous. Almost all were facing at least one significant life struggle—financial, physical, relational, career, etc.

3. Happy people laugh a lot—especially at themselves. They are rarely guilty of taking themselves too seriously.

4. Happy people don't depend on money or material possessions. They don't get their joy from luxury cars, yachts, mansions, private jets, vacation villas in Europe, or courtside seats to their favorite team's games.

5. Happy people are ridiculously unselfish. They give presents for no reason. They spring for lunch. They lend books, CDs, even their cars. In fact, we didn't hear of a single person who was truly happy but also greedy. The most joy-filled individuals are givers. They are all about serving others.

6. The happiest people alive happen to follow Jesus Christ. Not to say that all Christians are 100 percent cheerful all the time, but the owners of real joy don't try to manufacture it in their little home labs. They get the pure, natural stuff straight from the Source. They know that every good and perfect gift comes from God, and they are thankful for every one of those gifts.

7. Happy people know what they're doing here (obeying God and spreading love like it was creamy peanut butter). And they know when they are done here, they will go *there*. And they know when they get there, it will be heaven.

Joy is a gift from God, and it is much more than just a good feeling. Followers of Christ can experience joy when their circumstances stink, even during suffering. Even during the worst possible times, God gives us the ability to express genuine joy. Paul and his buddies were known for singing joyfully while chained together in disgusting prisons. (It's too bad "Unchained Melody" hadn't been written back then; we think Paul would have loved the irony of singing that one. "Chain of Fools" too.)

We don't mean to imply that there isn't a time for sorrow or mourning. Of course, the expression of pain has its place along our journey. But our final destination will certainly be joy. Our man C. S. Lewis said that the serious business of heaven will be joy. How cool will that be? Why not get a head start now?

While we're still on earth, we can know that joy is powerful and available. We simply need to ask for it and look for it.

Joy and laughter are all around us if we keep our eyes open. We're humans—we do goofy, ridiculous things all the time. Things we say we'll laugh about in ten years are probably funny right now. Who says we have to wait? Our friend Mark Lowry said it well: "God loves to hear his children laugh. What healthy father doesn't?" So don't hold back. Laugh. Chuckle. Titter, if you must. Guffaw if you can.

 **SLICE OF ADVICE:**

"Let your heart give you joy in the days of your youth" (Ecclesiastes 11:9).

 **DELIVER ON THIS:**

Look for opportunities to bring joy and laughter to yourself and others. Look for the humor in life. Give the gift of laughter to someone in need. You just might end up on somebody's happy list.

DON'T BELIEVE THE PARTY LINE ABOUT PARTIES

We had all these great ideas for this chapter about partying. We were going to be philosophical and balanced and take a position that was reasonable—but still made us look cool. Our basic theme was going to be something like "Party Smart" or "Go Ahead and Party, but Keep These Guidelines in Mind."

Then Jenna Cooper changed our minds, without saying a word. Actually, Jenna *can't* say a word because she died during the writing of this book. She was a beautiful, well-liked college student and soccer star. She was at a party when an argument broke out. She had nothing to do with the dispute, but, as it turns out, alcohol-fueled hotheads aren't the best shots. She was hit by a stray bullet and killed.

Wondering what the disagreement was about? Hoping that, at the very least, Jenna died as the result of an honorable dispute? Try this: Two partygoers were arguing about the whereabouts of some shot glasses. Just the kind of vital argument that is best solved by gunplay.

Reading about Jenna brought to mind other infamous parties we know of, parties that some of our friends attended. At two of them, girls were gang-raped. At another, a friend of ours overdosed and had to be held down by a half-dozen guys to keep him from killing himself or someone else. Then there was the time a guy was almost beaten to death. . . .

So much for being philosophical and balanced. Sorry, but we have to take the hard line on the party line. We can't think of *any* good reason for you to attend a party where alcohol, drugs, and/or guns are present. The same goes for a party without adult supervision. (And your friend's big brother, Reggie, the college dropout with two DUIs to his credit, doesn't qualify as an adult *or* a supervisor.)

We know the possible arguments: "I'll go, but I won't do any of that wild stuff." "I need to be there to keep my friends out of trouble." "I can set a good example by not doing drugs or drinking." We used these lines too. But here's what we learned.

First, if you're at a party or a rave where people get busted doing meth, Ecstasy, or whatever, you will be one of *dozens* of people who "weren't doing anything." Your excuse might be legit, but to a lot of people in authority it will sound like just one more half-baked excuse from just one more half-baked partier.

Second, if you're not going to the party to *party*, what's the point? That's kind of like going to the gym to watch the other people work out, or going to the All-You-Can-Eat Buffet to watch the other people eat.

Third, the intention to keep one's party-going friends from harm might be honorable, but it's not practical. If your friends tend to get intoxicated, it will be hard to reason with them. If they are going to a party to hook up, they will resent you if you get in the way. Please consider this: If you *really* want to keep your friends from getting messed up at a party, shouldn't you keep them from *going* to the party in the first place?

Fourth, good luck trying to set a good example for a bunch of drunk, high, and/or horny teens. They will either ignore you or be too messed up to take note of you or your fine, upstanding example. To follow the line of reasoning in the paragraph above: If you really want to set a good party-related example, tell people *beforehand*—while they are still coherent—that you won't be attending the party—and why.

A final thought on the subject: We recently heard a friend bragging, "I got so wasted at this party! Everyone was so trashed!" It never ceases to amaze us to hear people boast about likening themselves to discarded refuse. Think about the terms associated with partying—many of which we can't even mention because of our publisher's high literary standards: Trashed. Messed up. Bleep-faced. Baked. Stoned. Wasted.

The terms should tell you something. Spending your time and money poisoning your mind, watching your friends debase themselves, risking your health and reputation? What a waste.

 ## SLICE OF ADVICE:

"The acts of the sinful nature are obvious: sexual immorality, impurity and debauchery ... drunkenness, orgies, and the like. I warn you ... those who live like this will not inherit the kingdom of God" (Galatians 5:19, 21).

 ## DOUBLE SLICE OF ADVICE:

1. Get an accountability partner who will keep you away from parties. If you insist on going to wild parties (which we firmly believe is a mistake), at the very least, bring another sober person along so that the two of you can keep yourselves accountable and out of trouble.
2. Get with some creative friends and plan your own party—one free of vomit, intoxication, guns, illegal drugs, fights, and, in general, things people will (or should be)

ashamed of later. And we're not talking about playing Pin the Tail on the Donkey or Musical Chairs. We said to be creative, remember? Plan with a clear, creative, joyful mind. Then party the same way.

HOW WELL CAN YOU RELATE?

Human relationships will never be perfect until we all get to Heaven. Until that day, our interactions with family and friends will be sources of great joy, but also extreme frustration and even deep pain.

God created relationships and gave us the perfect model of how they should look. We were meant to love each other, to serve each other, and to put others' needs ahead of our own.

The world's version of relationship is, quite often, selfish. Think about how many times you've been asked, "What do you look for in a friend?" "What's your idea of the perfect date?" Have you *ever* been asked, "What do you hope you can bring to your friendships?" "What kind of boyfriend or girlfriend do you aspire to be?" Did those last two questions seem odd? Thank the twenty-first century's mantra: *All me, all the time.* Have you *ever* heard of anyone ending a romance or a friendship by saying, "I don't think *I* was bringing enough to our relationship. I wasn't doing enough for *you*"? Nope, it's all about "What's in it for me?" "What have you done for me lately?" "Are you meeting *my* needs?"

Is it any wonder that we tend to approach relationships with suspicious eyes, half-closed hearts, or worse—a "get them before they get you" attitude?

God did not intend for us to live in this bizarre relationship economy, in which we try to gain as much as we can from others while giving as little as we can get away with.

A friendship, romance, or family relationship built on that economic model is going to bankrupt some people before long. Relationships work best under God's model. If we, with an open heart, love each other, serve each other, and put our own selfish agenda last on the list, we reap big hefty bushels of love and joy in return. Does this sound like a paradox? It is. Welcome to the Christian faith, an entire way of life built on paradox. A small seed becomes a huge tree. Those who are willing to fall in at the end of the line end up getting upgraded to the front. Give stuff away like there's no tomorrow and you get it back with interest. Clutch on to stuff with a Kung-Fu grip and it'll whither and die and slip right out of your hands. Serve people humbly and you'll become a leader.

What does this have to do with your relationship with your parents, siblings, friends, and romantic interest? Simple—if you are keeping score with any of the above people, you are playing the wrong game!

We urge you to put away the scorecards when it comes to your relationships. Start asking yourself questions like, "What can I bring to the table in my relationships?" "What needs do those around me have—and how can I help meet them?" "What can I do that will delight the people in my life? Surprise them? Honor them? Show them God's love?"

We promise you that this approach, the one Jesus modeled so well, will set you free—turn you loose to be the kind of friend, son, daughter, sibling, boyfriend, girlfriend, whatever, that people will thank God for.

Wouldn't you like to play the relationship game this way, not the world's way? If so, it's your turn to serve.

SLICE OF ADVICE:

"Serve one another in love" (Galatians 5:13).

DELIVER ON THIS:

Get rid of anything that tempts you to "keep score" in your relationships. And stop yourself any time you find yourself doing it. Don't worry about whose turn it is to buy gas or who sprung for lunch last time or who owes whom a phone call or e-mail. Buy your best friend the birthday present you *want* to buy—don't obsess over how much he or she spent on your present. Don't stress over which sibling gets the most time on the computer.

If you quit keeping score in your relationships, everyone can win. If you quit comparing everything, your relationships will be incomparable.

GOOD GRIEF: OXYMORON OR REALITY?

W e live in a fallen world, and as a result, we all experience pain. The hurt of a loved one lost will affect every one of us at some point. That's sobering news, but here's some good news to balance it: The pain, the questions, the helpless feelings—God is Lord over all of it.

He never said our journey would be without heartaches, without loss. From our earthly perspective, the death of a loved one is devastating in its apparent finality. Yet from God's eternal, all-knowing perspective, it's just a temporary separation.

This is not to say that he doesn't hurt with us and for us. Remember the famous "shortest verse in the Bible"? John 11:35 says "Jesus wept." Why did he cry?

In the story, Jesus' good friend Lazarus died and Jesus arrived at the burial site. Jesus knew that in a few seconds he was going to tell Lazarus to rise up and come out of his tomb. Yet he still cried. He was deeply moved.

Why? Did the fully human aspect of Jesus simply miss his friend? Or were his tears more for Lazarus's friends and family—tears of empathy? Maybe it was a combination of both.

God knows when you are hurting, and he feels the hurt right along with you. That is something we can take comfort in. When we hurt, finding someone who understands allows us to be open with our emotions. We don't have to worry about being looked at as if we are crazy. We can be honest, authentic before God.

Of course, God is more than empathetic and understanding. He is loving, wise, all-powerful, and eternal. This means that, someday, we will see his whole plan and how he orchestrated it all through history. We'll see that he was beside us, loving us and working through us, even in our times of heartbreak.

For now, we can rest in the understanding that God's plan is good; he wants to give us a future filled with hope, and he will make good on his promise to work all things for our good if we love and serve him. This doesn't mean that everything that happens in our lives will be good. It wasn't good for us when our grandfather died, when our mom died, when some of our close friends died. But God was our comfort and our hope in those times. And he did bring good from those tragedies. Family bonds were strengthened. Friendships were rekindled. Priorities were put in their proper order.

This world can hurt sometimes. If you have lost someone you love, we truly feel for you. And we ask that, even through your tears, you try to look ahead with hope. This world is not our home. Heaven is a real place and we will see it—and all its citizens—soon enough. Then we will grieve no more.

We aren't going to lie to you: Grief is a weight you might have to carry for a long time. But thank God, you don't have to carry it alone.

SLICE OF ADVICE:

It's worth remembering that death ends a life on earth. It doesn't have to end a relationship. It doesn't negate the goodness and affection that a deceased loved one poured into your life. It doesn't erase the memories. And, most important, death is not final. It's a temporary condition. Thank heaven for that.

DELIVER ON THIS:

If you have lost someone close to you, write the person a letter. Really. This is something we learned at a church-based Grief Recovery workshop, and it's a deeply meaningful exercise. Tell the person how much you miss him or her; reminisce about favorite times together. Talk about what you learned as a result of your relationship. Share actions you will take to help keep his or her memory—and legacy—alive. This task is hard and painful, but truly rewarding when you are done. And in some mysterious way, it helps raw, open wounds begin to heal.

Additionally, no matter how prepared you are for a loved one's death, there isn't enough time to share all the thoughts and emotions. Doing it in a letter can bring a sense of peace and remove the pangs of regret that many of us feel when we lose someone we love.

CONGRATULATIONS— YOU'RE GIFTED!

You are a gifted person—truly. It doesn't matter what your report cards or I.Q. tests say. You have spiritual gifts. We wouldn't lie to you. Spiritual gifts are like nostrils—everybody has a couple (at least), and we all need to use them.

Too many times we figure that we're nothing special and God must've given all the cool abilities to everybody else.

We need to stop selling God short and thinking he got stingy when it came to us. So you can't part the Red Sea, big deal. We can barely part our *hair*. Still, the Bible tells us clearly that *all* of us have been given gifts and we need to use them in accordance with our faith.

When we consider the many different gifts listed in the Bible, it's easy to see why Paul compares the body of believers to a physical body with many different parts serving many different functions. Just like a human body, the body of Christ (the church) needs all those parts to function properly. Even the little toe. Don't believe us? An acquaintance of ours actually—and accidentally—shot off his little toe. He had to relearn how to walk, and it took a *long* time. And while he suffered through this process, the lack of a toe caused pain in his foot, leg, and clear up to his back and neck as other body parts tried to compensate for the lack of that one little three-quarter-inch appendage.

You might think yourself small and insignificant, but the body of Christ would be hurtin' without you.

See, not only did God create you as a unique being, he also entrusted you with a unique set of abilities to serve specific purposes within His plan. He made you with special work in mind.

From encouraging to healing, from leadership to giving, from interpreting dreams to teaching, there is tremendous variety in the gifts discussed in the Bible and, trust us, you have some of those abilities. You just might not know it yet.

Just like athletes who may be born with certain natural abilities, we must discover, build, and fine-tune in order to maximize our Spirit skills. Most important, we must develop our gifts by *using* them!

For example, your ability to lead—to inspire and direct others through words and example—is like a muscle. You can strengthen your leadership muscles every time you learn from a leader you admire and put his or her principles into practice. Like a muscle, faith (belief) can get stronger and so can our ability to use this gift. That's the cool thing about spiritual gifts—they get better and more valuable to those around us as we put them into action.

Have you already discovered some of your spiritual gifts? If so, are you using them? If you haven't discovered these gifts yet, take heart. We're about to help you. Again, you have some, as sure as you're breathing through your nostrils right now.

SLICE OF ADVICE:

"Follow the way of love and eagerly desire spiritual gifts" (1 Corinthians 14:1).

DELIVER ON THIS:

Following is a list of spiritual gifts (taken from 1 Corinthians 12 and Romans 12). Look the list over. Do you recognize some of these gifts—or the potential for them—in yourself? If so, start building them and putting them into practice. If you need additional guidance on this topic, consult your pastor or youth leader. He or she might have a questionnaire or other tool to help you determine your specific gifts.

SPIRITUAL GIFTS

Service: This can include serving your church or community in a number of ways. This kind of service can also include a church office, such as deacon.

Wisdom/Knowledge: You don't have to be wrinkly and bearded to be wise. (This should be especially good news to you girls.) The gifts of wisdom and knowledge can enable a person to help others make sound decisions and choose the best course of action.

Faith: This doesn't mean "saving faith," the faith we put in God to save us from the consequences of our sin. This particular breed of faith is an especially strong trust in God and his wisdom and ability to provide for our needs. Some Bible translations describe this gift as "wonder-working faith" or "great faith." In your case, it might be your ability to help others maintain perspective in difficult times—helping them avoid becoming discouraged or angry.

Healing: It's unfortunate that various religious hucksters have cheapened this gift's reputation. But the truth remains: The Bible says that the prayer of a righteous person can accomplish many things, and that includes healing various illnesses. We are convinced that our grandfather's severe cancer went into remission for seven years as the result of prayers by a person or people with the gift of healing. We believe that a relative's prayer kept Todd's daughter Olivia alive during a near-miscarriage. (And we are notorious skeptics about this kind of thing.)

Miraculous Powers: Sorry, but this doesn't mean that God will turn you into Spider-Man or Elektra. But it does mean that God can work through certain people to accomplish tasks that might not have been possible by natural means.

Prophecy: This is another misunderstood gift. It isn't all about predicting who will win the next Super Bowl or the next installment of *Survivor*. Don't go up to a person with the spiritual gift of prophecy and ask for next week's lottery numbers. Prophecy is more about "forth-telling" than foretelling. In other words, a prophet's most important duty is discerning God's will in a particular matter or situation and making that will known to others.

Distinguishing Between Spirits: If you can cut through smoke and hype, separate substance from flash, you might have this gift. Every day we are bombarded by self-serving messages and dangerous lies masquerading as spiritual truth. If you have this gift, we need you to unmask deception and uphold the truth.

Speaking in Different Tongues/Interpreting Tongues: This is a controversial set of gifts. The first part of this gift refers to a person's being able to speak an unlearned human language, through the power of God's spirit. Some theologians also believe that this gift includes the ability to speak in "heavenly languages," including worshipful languages of praise and prayer to God. The second part of this gift refers to the ability to understand these different languages and communicate their meaning to others. This is an important point: If someone speaks in a strange language in church, for example, and no one can decipher what he or she is saying, everyone in the congregation hears only gibberish and can't be edified or challenged or comforted by the message.

Teaching: The ability to explain spiritual truths and biblical principles in an engaging, effective, memorable way. Different teachers can be effective with different age groups, so don't be discouraged if your peer group seems unteachable. You might have a knack for connecting with a younger age group.

Encouraging: This one is self-explanatory. If you have a knack for lifting people up when they are feeling low, this gift is probably yours.

Giving/Contributing: A lot of people don't see this as a gift. God does. This gift includes not only the ability and generosity to give your own time and resources but to help others do the same—and organize charity programs and events.

Mercy: You probably didn't know this was a spiritual gift either, did you? But it's a cool one. Think of how many people can benefit from the gift of compassion, shown through encouraging words, a warm hug, a gift of food or money to someone in need.

Leadership: You don't have to be a CEO of a Christian company or the senior pastor of a megachurch to use this gift. You can be a leader in your youth group, even just your circle of friends. Advise. Encourage. Set an example.

No matter who you are, we are confident that at least a couple of the gifts above resonate with you. So unwrap them. Use them. They're yours to share with your world.

FINAL REHEAT

Okay, it's time to give the microwave one final spin . . .

1. When it comes to temptation, become a freestyle fleeing champion. Watch your weak spots—that's where evil is going to try to tag you.

2. Joyful people are giving people. Some say "Give till it hurts." We say, "Give till it's hilarious."

3. You gotta fight for your right *not* to party.

4. Don't keep score in your relationships. When you do that, everybody loses.

5. Grief is one of life's painful realities. But grief, like even death itself, is only temporary. Thank God for that.

6. You are spiritually talented and gifted—with the kind of gifts that keep on giving!

WHO WANTS TO BE THE NEXT, NEXT, NEXT BIG THING?

Congratulations! You've almost finished all of your pizza! We thank you for sharing this "soul food" with us. We hope you've picked up a few new insights—and been reminded of some others.

We encourage you to re-read chapters that have been particularly meaningful or challenging for you. We do this with books all the time. We find that we learn something new or understand something better the second time—or third time—around. Besides, we love C. S. Lewis's definition of an illiterate: "Someone who reads a book only once."

We welcome your e-mails. We want to know what worked for you, what didn't work, and, most important, how we can pray for you, support you. Hit us back via our Web site, *www.haferbros.com.*

We want to leave you with a few final thoughts on the subject of finding true success and meaning in life. We hear a lot of theories about what constitutes success; you probably do too. We don't like the flavor of today's success formulas.

Here's the twenty-first century's largest and loudest success message: "You have to make it big. You have to win!" TV has turned everything into a contest. Programs like *American Karaoke* (oops, we mean *American Idol*) show us that it is not enough to entertain, you have to be *the* entertainer. You have to beat the other entertainers.

And the phenomenon doesn't stop at entertainment. Getting a job, realizing your dream, finding a date, finding a mate—it's all been turned into a contest. Even finding a mate for your *dad* has been turned into a competition!

Adults, teens, and even kids are affected. If you're a grade-schooler, it's not enough to play soccer or tennis anymore—you have to "play up" against athletes older, bigger, and more experienced than you. Listening to National Public Radio recently, we heard a report noting that athletes as young as eleven were taking steroids in an ill-conceived quest to achieve an edge over their competitors.

When we were teens, we Hafer brothers bought into this philosophy. We both had bedrooms that were essentially shrines to athletic achievement. Varsity letters, tournament brackets, award certificates, newspaper clippings, photos, ribbons, and medals covered our walls. We had transformed our humble rooms into Shrines of Sweat. Too much of our self-esteem came from what hung from the walls, not what was in our hearts.

We relied on the awards to impress girls too. Took the pressure off of us to be kind, thoughtful, charming—and all of that burdensome stuff.

Where are all of those prized possessions—those monuments to athletic achievement—today? We have no idea. Do we miss them? Nope. Are we even a bit curious as to their whereabouts? Not even a little.

Why? Because we've learned a lot about what constitutes true success. We are still learning, but as we wrapped up this book, we thought of six things we wish we had known about true success. We share these with you now.

1. Your best accomplishments in life—the ones that are most rewarding to you and others, the ones you will be remembered

for—will come to you when you are serving others, following Jesus' example. Jesus spelled success S-E-R-V-E.

2. People matter to God and to the world. You matter. You are a custom-designed person with good works just begging to be done. God has equipped you to make unique contributions to the world. Nobody can do the specific good works—in the trademark way—that you can. And God has blessings with *your* name on them. He doesn't send blessings addressed to "Occupant." You might have prayed to God to send a person into your life to revolutionize it. Your prayer has been answered. That "person" is you!

3. Don't let the world—especially the media—force you into a mold. Be real. Be you. You have a unique vision, a unique voice. In the history of the universe, there has never been anyone quite like you. So don't be anybody's wannabe—not for money, not for fame, and especially not for love and acceptance. The person you truly are is more interesting and lovable than whoever you might pretend to be.

4. True success in life comes from loving what you do. Don't do anything for the money or the fame or the prestige or the public approval. Don't strive to merely make a salary or make a grade. Make a difference. The world has more than enough movie stars, music monoliths, media moguls, and millionaires. The world has a ridiculous surplus of celebrities. It could use a few more honest-to-God saints. Are you game?

5. Don't sell out, no matter what. You will be tempted; that's almost a guarantee. Don't compromise your principles. Don't lie or cheat or take the low road—not for money or attention or sex or anything else. Selling out becomes a habit. You lose a true sense of who you are—and Whom you belong to. You wake up one day and you're just a hollow shell of a person. And there's nothing left to do but rent yourself out as a canoe.

6. You are going to hear many loud voices, urging you to Make the Big Bucks, Climb the Ladder, Find the Hottie, Seek the Thrill. We have a few alternate suggestions. Savor the life. Love the people. Serve the people. Walk with Jesus.

EXTRA TOPPINGS (AT NO EXTRA CHARGE!)

e invite you to check out this little bonus section. You might find something worth tossing on your *Pizza*.

MORE STUFF TO CHEW ON

These are books that have challenged us, energized us, comforted us, inspired us. We hope they'll do the same for you.

Also, we're interested in the books on *your* all-time, desert-island reading list. E-mail us, and maybe we can include your recommendations in our next serving of "Pizza."

Apologetics/Key Biblical Truths

The Case for a Creator (Student Edition) by Lee Strobel. Embark on a journey into the origin of the universe and discover scientific proof for the Intelligent Designer behind it all. Strobel presents this compelling case as only a Yale Law School–educated newspaper editor—and former religious skeptic—can.

Evidence That Demands a Verdict and *New Evidence That Demands a Verdict* by Josh McDowell. For many people, these books are *the* apologetics classics. Have doubts about the Bible's origins and reliability? Or about whether a man named Jesus really walked the earth, died, and rose again? Consider the Evidence. And for a dedicated focus on the Son of God, check out McDowell's *More Than a Carpenter*.

The Holiness of God by R. C. Sproul. Sproul is one of our dad's favorite contemporary theologians, and he's become one of ours as well. Most people understand that God is loving and powerful. But holy? What exactly does that mean, and how does it affect our relationship with our Creator? Check this book out; you'll be wholly inspired.

Letters From a Skeptic by Gregory and Edward Boyd. What a cool idea for a book. A pastor corresponds with his atheist father about the key truths of the Christian faith. The senior Mr. Boyd fires tough questions like fastballs. His son doesn't duck a single one. He stands in the intellectual batter's box and faces each challenge with logic, warmth, and respect. This may be the best-ever depiction of apologetics applied to contemporary life.

Mere Christianity by C. S. Lewis. You can't go wrong with any of Lewis's books, but this one is our favorite. Here, you'll find the case for Christianity stated in a way that's compelling to your mind and your heart.

Blue Like Jazz by Donald Miller. Think all Christians are right-wing political and religious conservatives? Think all Christian writers are theological giants who never doubt or question? Think that evidence of God can't be found in odd topics like penguin sex? Read this book and think again.

God Thinks You're Wonderful by Max Lucado. We put Mr. Lucado in the same camp as C. S. Lewis. Every book he's done is a winner. This one is a great choice, especially for newcomers to Camp Lucado, because it's a quick read that offers bite-sized thoughts from many of Lucado's bestselling books.

Jesus Freaks (Volumes 1 & 2) by dc Talk and the Voice of the Martyrs. We sometimes feel bad when our faith gets us made fun of at work or denied media coverage. Then we read these books, about people whose faith cost them much more—even, in some cases, their lives. Then we feel ashamed—but also inspired. You will too. Get your Freak on.

The Unrandom Universe: How Science Can Strengthen Your Faith by Sigmund Brouwer. Sigmund is one of the brightest contemporary minds, and he is a truly gifted writer. This book is one of the best around when it comes to dispelling the myth that science and creationism are mortal enemies.

Applying Faith to Everyday Life

Disappointment with God by Philip Yancey. This book is subtitled *Three Questions No One Asks Aloud.* These are questions—and answers—worth checking out.

The GodSpeaks Devotional (various contributors). Based on those famous billboards with quotes attributed to God, this edgy, practical book reveals much about God's character and his expectations of his followers. (Plus, you can play a detective game with this book; read through it and try to determine which quotes and accompanying devotions the Hafer brothers wrote.)

In the Grip of Grace by Max Lucado. Here, Lucado clearly explains the magnitude of God's grace—and how we should respond to that grace.

It's Not About Me by Max Lucado. Just in case you thought it was about you, here's a reality check. The funny thing is, this book portrays the biblical truth that when you give your life up to a cause greater than yourself, you find personal fulfillment that you'd never realize otherwise.

The Life You've Always Wanted by John Ortberg. Life can be so much more fulfilling when we pursue God's priorities, as opposed to chasing the "fetch sticks" the world tries to get us to scurry after. This book is filled with godly wisdom and wonderful, real-life examples of living the abundant life God desires for his children.

The Purpose-Driven Life by Rick Warren. There's a reason this book has sold more than seventeen million copies. Life was designed to be lived on purpose, and Warren helps readers understand, embrace, and live out that purpose.

The Ragamuffin Gospel by Brennan Manning. A beautiful, honest portrait of humanity's weakness and the strength of God's grace. This book is like a super-size, bladder-busting cup of pure, undiluted, industrial-strength grace. Take a big gulp. Take several big gulps. Chug the whole thing, because this grace stuff comes in unlimited refills.

CONTEMPORARY ISSUES

In the Chat Room With God and *Stranger in the Chat Room* by Todd and Jedd Hafer. What kind of knuckleheads would be presumptuous enough to recommend their own books? Well, "the kind of knuckleheads we are" is the answer here. We received a lot of great feedback on these books, and no, all of it *wasn't* from relatives or people who owe us money. The "Chat Room" books address contemporary issues in a format we hope you'll find intriguing.

Dateable and *The Dateable Rules* by Justin Lookadoo and Hayley Morgan. Some important truths about dating. Both "Dateables" are very readable. You'll better understand the opposite sex (but keep in mind that this is a lifelong process). The books will help you make dating choices based on biblical principles, not modeling the dating regimens of someone like Paris Hilton.

Time for a Pure Revolution by Doug Herman. This book isn't just about keeping yourself pure sexually. In the author's words, it's also about "life restored to its original point. That means we need pure relationships, where families will once again truly connect and communicate. We need schools where pure education addresses all issues of life. . . . And we need the church to wake up and understand why we believe what we believe and to teach it rationally, relationally, and respectfully."

MORE WORDS FROM THE WORD

We liberally sprinkled *Wake Up and Smell the Pizza* with Scripture verses. However, there are many that we couldn't squeeze in before, so we want to provide them here, as an additional resource for you. (You'll also note that we've repeated a few verses we believe might be extra significant for you. We've organized the verses under various headings to help you find what you need, when those late-night Bible-verse cravings hit.)

GOD'S CHARACTER

God is faithful, by whom ye were called unto the fellowship of his Son Jesus Christ our Lord. 1 Corinthians 1:9 KJV

Do not fear, for I am with you; do not be dismayed, for I am your God. I will strengthen you . . . with my righteous right hand. Isaiah 41:10

The Lord saw how great man's wickedness on earth had become . . . his heart was only evil all the time. The Lord was grieved that he had made man on the earth, and his heart was filled with pain. Genesis 6:5–6

Blessed be the Lord your God, who delighted in you. 1 Kings 10:9 NKJV

Never will I leave you; never will I forsake you. Hebrews 13:5

The Lord is watching his children, listening to their prayers. 1 Peter 3:12 TLB

GOD'S FAITHFULNESS

There shall not any man be able to stand before thee all the days of thy life: as I was with Moses, so I will be with thee: I will not fail thee, nor forsake thee. Joshua 1:5 KJV

Those who hope in the Lord will renew their strength. They will soar on wings like eagles; they will run and not grow weary, they will walk and not be faint. Isaiah 40:31

GOD'S LOVE AND CARE FOR HIS PEOPLE

My grace is sufficient for thee: for my strength is made perfect in weakness. 2 Corinthians 12:9 KJV

The Lord will guide you always; he will satisfy your needs. Isaiah 58:11

I have come that they may have life, and that they may have it more abundantly. John 10:10 NKJV

My sheep recognize my voice, and I know them, and they follow me. I give them eternal life and they shall never perish. No one shall snatch them away from me. John 10:27–28 TLB

You created my inmost being; you knit me together in my mother's womb. I praise you because I am fearfully and wonderfully made. Psalm 139:13–14

Come to me, all you who are weary and burdened, and I will give you rest. Matthew 11:28

PERSPECTIVE

And we know that in all things God works for the good of those who love him, who have been called according to His purpose. Romans 8:28

A cheerful heart is good medicine. Proverbs 17:22

Don't worry about anything; instead, pray about everything; tell God your needs, and don't forget to thank him for his answers. If you do this, you will experience God's peace, which is far more wonderful than the human mind can understand. His peace will keep your thoughts and your hearts quiet and at rest as you trust in Christ Jesus. Philippians 4:6–7 TLB

Cast your cares on the Lord and he will sustain you. Psalm 55:22

Where your treasure is, there your heart will be also. Matthew 6:21

Be joyful in hope, patient in affliction, faithful in prayer. Romans 12:12

Therefore I tell you, do not worry about your life, what you will eat. . . . Life is more than food. Luke 12:22–23

THE BIBLE AND ITS POWER

Your word is a lamp to my feet and a light for my path. Psalm 119:105

HUMANITY'S RESPONSIBILITY TO GOD

Love the Lord your God with all your heart and with all your soul and with all your strength. Deuteronomy 6:5

Remember your Creator in the days of your youth. Ecclesiastes 12:1

What does the Lord require of you? To act justly and to love mercy and to walk humbly with your God. Micah 6:8

Do not neglect your gift. 1 Timothy 4:14

If you love me, you will obey what I command. John 14:15

Whatever you do, work at it with all your heart, as working for the Lord, not for men. Colossians 3:23

Let us not give up meeting together, as some are in the habit of doing, but let us encourage one another—and all the more as you see the Day approaching. Hebrews 10:25

As God's chosen people, holy and dearly loved, clothe yourselves with compassion, kindness, humility, gentleness and patience. Colossians 3:12

TRUE SUCCESS

What good will it be for a man if he gains the whole world, yet forfeits his soul? Matthew 16:26

The memory of the righteous will be a blessing, but the name of the wicked will rot. Proverbs 10:7

Be on your guard against all kinds of greed; a man's life does not consist in the abundance of his possessions. Luke 12:15

Whoever wishes to become great among you shall be your servant. Matthew 20:26 NASB

A good name is to be chosen rather than great riches, Loving favor rather than silver and gold. Proverbs 22:1 NKJV

INNER PEACE

Do not let your hearts be troubled. Trust in God; trust also in me. John 14:1

Do not be anxious about anything, but in everything, by prayer and petition, with thanksgiving, present your requests to God. Philippians 4:6

FORGIVENESS

I will forgive their wickedness and will remember their sins no more. Hebrews 8:12

LOVE

Do everything in love. 1 Corinthians 16:14

A new command I give you: Love one another. As I have loved you, so you must love one another. John 13:34

Above all, love each other deeply, because love covers over a multitude of sins. 1 Peter 4:8

Dear friends, let us love one another, for love comes from God. 1 John 4:7

Whoever does not love does not know God, because God is love. 1 John 4:8

If we love one another, God lives in us and his love is made complete in us. 1 John 4:12

LIVING IN HARMONY WITH OTHERS

Be patient with each other, making allowance for each other's faults because of your love. Ephesians 4:2 TLB

Accept one another, then, just as Christ accepted you, in order to bring praise to God. Romans 15:7

Honor one another above yourselves. Romans 12:10

Be compassionate and humble. 1 Peter 3:8

Bear with each other and forgive whatever grievances you may have against one another. Forgive as the Lord forgave you. Colossians 3:13

If you spend yourselves in behalf of the hungry and satisfy the needs of the oppressed, then your light will rise in the darkness, and your night will become like the noonday. Isaiah 58:10

If you are angry, don't sin by nursing your grudge. Ephesians 4:26 TLB

Live in peace with each other. 1 Thessalonians 5:13

Blessed are the merciful, for they will be shown mercy. Matthew 5:7

Be kind to one another, tenderhearted, forgiving one another, as God in Christ forgave you. Ephesians 4:32 RSV

HEAVEN: YOUR FUTURE HOME

And God shall wipe away all tears from their eyes; and there shall be no more death, neither sorrow, nor crying, neither shall there be any more pain: for the former things are passed away. Revelation 21:4 KJV

Whoever lives and believes in me will never die. John 11:26

Our citizenship is in heaven. And we eagerly await a Savior from there, the Lord Jesus Christ. Philippians 3:20

FOOTNOTES

AIDS and STDs: Statistics are from a B&B Media Group press release about Doug Herman's "Pure Revolution" radio program. According to the release, AIDS is the leading cause of death among people 25 to 44, and about 4 million teens are infected with STDs each year.

Cheating and car ownership: Figures are from the publication *Men's Car,* as reported in the June 21, 2004, issue of *Newsweek.* (Fifty percent of Porsche owners admit to cheating on their partners, as do 46 percent of BMW owners.)

Deaths due to school-related violence: Statistics are from *USA Today,* June 28, 2004, issue. (The 48 school-related violent deaths during the 2003–2004 school year were the highest in the past decade. For comparison, during the 2002–2003 school year, the death total was 17.)

Internet illegal file sharing: Stats are from the July 12, 2004, issue of *USA Today.* A cover story notes that during the month of June 2004, 8.3 million people were online at a given time and using unauthorized file-sharing services.

Internet pornography: Information is from the July 12, 2004, issue of *Newsweek.* In a story on marital infidelity, *Newsweek* notes that the Internet boasts 4 million pornographic sites. In a related story, the July 12, 2004, issue of *USA Today* notes that pornography (videos and still images) represents more than 20 percent of all online file sharing, second only to music.

Marital infidelity: Statistics are from the July 12, 2004, issue of *Newsweek*. In this issue's cover story, couples therapists estimate that 30 to 40 percent of married women have affairs, compared with 50 percent of men. However, in the same story, direct surveys of men and women yielded different results. When the National Opinion Research Center at the University of Chicago asked men and women if they'd ever had sex outside their marriage, 15 percent of women and 22 percent of men said yes. Interestingly, the same survey indicates that 80 percent of Americans agree with the statement "infidelity is always wrong."

Millennials (those born in 1984 or later) leaving the church: Research by George Barna, as reported in the July 2004 issue of *CBA Marketplace*.

Parents still number-one influence on their kids' lives: Conclusion of Lawrence Kutner, Ph.D., child psychologist and teacher. Reported in the brochure "Raising Kids Who Don't Smoke," copyright 2003 by Philip Morris USA.

Robert Redford quotes: These are gleaned from interviews on National Public Radio, *Crankycritic.com,* and a TV interview that we turned on in progress and didn't get the name of the show. Sorry 'bout that.

Teenage smoking statistics: Gleaned from "Raising Kids Who Don't Smoke," copyright 2003 by Philip Morris USA. According to this publication, 26.7 percent of American twelfth graders reported smoking a cigarette within the past 30 days. More than 20 percent of high school students report that they smoked a cigarette before age 13. (Not to get off on too much of a tangent about smoking, but you should know that every year, more Americans die from cigarette-related illnesses than alcohol, car accidents, suicide, AIDS, homicide, and illegal drugs combined. And don't think you're safe just because you don't smoke. Second-hand smoke contains 43 chemicals that are known to cause cancer.)

Teen suicide: According to research from the National Centers for Disease Control, suicide is the third-leading cause of death among young people ages 15 to 24. Males account for 86 percent of the suicides in this age group.

PIZZA TO YOUR EARS

We love Christian books, and we are voracious readers. We're usually each reading several books at a time, which is a real challenge for a couple of guys with limited intellectual capacity. But we simply must read, just as we must eat. (Lots.) Because authors have shaped our thoughts on key subjects, they've answered some questions, but more important, raised many more. We wouldn't be writing books ourselves if not for the wisdom and inspiration of people like Charles Colson, R. C. Sproul, Frederick Buechner, Francis Schaeffer, C. S. Lewis, Max Lucado, Anne Lamott, J. I. Packer, Martin Luther, Billy Graham, Madeleine L'Engle, Elizabeth Barrett Browning, Brennan Manning, and many others.

But we are inspired by great music too. And some of the most profound truths we hear come from songs, not the pages of a book. So we want to thank and honor the many artists who formed the soundtrack for this book's creation. These are the people who fed us at 3:30 A.M, when we needed to finish one more chapter before we could sleep.

These are the people who crafted lyrics so meaningful that we had to pull off the road and jot down the thoughts they inspired when we heard their songs on the car CD player or radio.

Some of the names below aren't just artists to us. Some we are grateful to call friends. For this, we are blessed beyond belief. This list represents only a fraction of our combined CD collection; we don't mean to omit anyone. These are simply the people who inspired and challenged and encouraged us while we created this book. We offer their names in the hope that they might do something similar for you, the reader.

Burlap to Cashmere
Caedmon's Call
Eva Cassidy
Steven Curtis Chapman
The Choir
dc Talk
GRITS
Jars of Clay
Rachel Lampa
Lifehouse
Maria McKee
MercyMe
Rich Mullins
Nichole Nordeman
O.C. Supertones
Danny Oertli
Stacie Orrico
Pillar
P.O.D.
Relient K
Sixpence None the Richer
Skillet
Michael W. Smith
Rebecca St. James
Switchfoot
Superchic(k)
Steve Taylor
Third Day
Tallon Trammell

ACKNOWLEDGMENTS

This book would not exist without the many friends and colleagues who graciously shared with us their insights, encouragement, and support. Many of the topics covered in *Pizza* are a direct result of our conversations with these people—and the inspiration we have experienced through their CDs, books, articles, sermons, etc.

So a super-supreme-with-extra-toppings thanks to . . .

Everyone at Bethany House Publishers, especially Natasha Sperling and Kyle Duncan for sharing our vision for reaching today's teens with God's truth.

Scott Degelman

Dr. Charles Fay of the Love and Logic Institute

The Reverend Del "Pops" Hafer of Cornerstone Presbyterian Church

Bradd and Chadd Hafer (our bros)

Pastor Matt Heard of Woodmen Valley Chapel

Bruce Hirakawa

Pat Judd (thanks for the doors you've opened)

Toby Mac

Chip MacGregor and the staff at Alive Communications

Nichole Nordeman (our longtime bud and favorite former Red Robin hostess)

Danny Oertli

Stacie Orrico (Thanks for taking the time to share what today's teens are telling you.)

Steve Riach, of The Heart of a Champion Foundation

Valerie Schroeder Skaret (We are proud of you, little sister!)

The members of Superchic(k), especially Max Hsu and Tricia and Melissa Brock (Siblings rock!)

Steve Taylor, creative genius (and fellow gangly PK)